1998 | World
Bank
Atlas

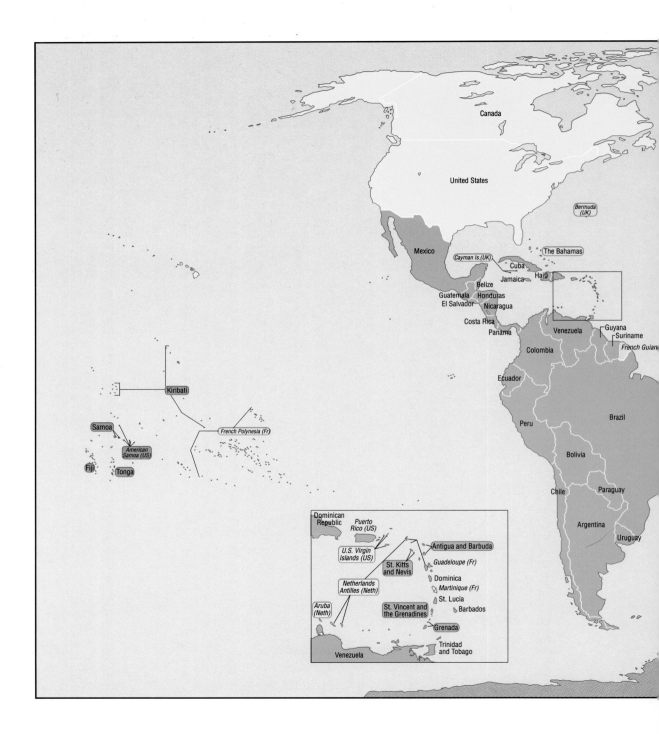

Low- and middle-income economies

- East Asia and the Pacific
- Europe and Central Asia
- Latin America and the Caribbean
- Middle East and North Africa
- South Asia
- Sub-Saharan Africa

High-income economies

- OECD
- Other

- No data

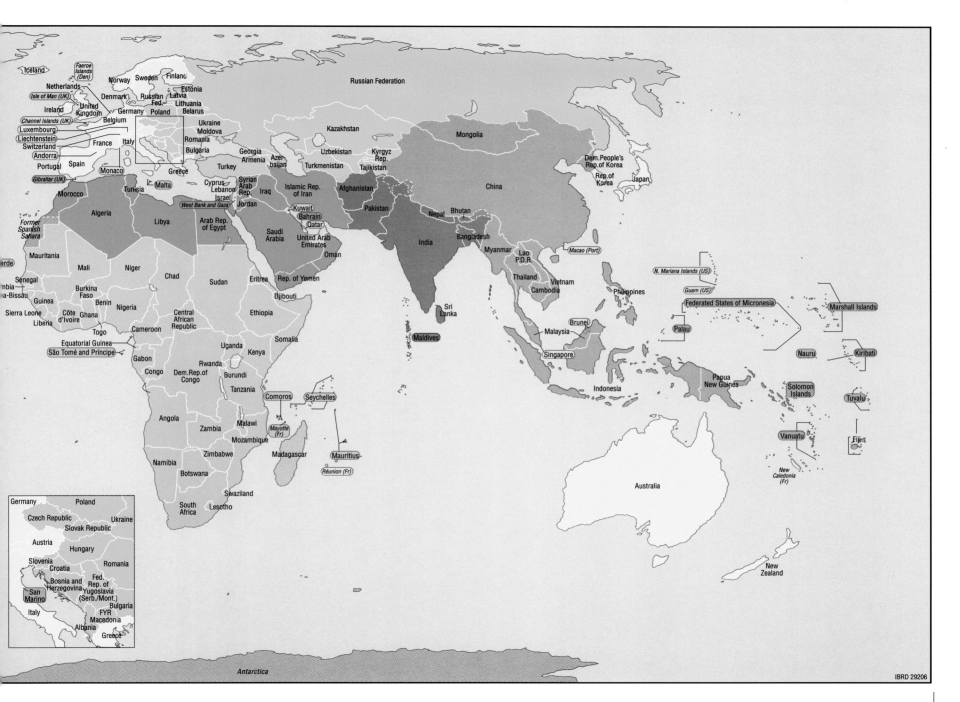

Iceland
Faeroe Islands (Den)
Norway   Sweden   Finland
Netherlands
Isle of Man (UK)
Ireland
Channel Islands (UK)
United Kingdom
Denmark
Germany
Belgium
Luxembourg
Liechtenstein
Switzerland
Andorra
France
Italy
Portugal   Spain
Gibraltar (UK)
Monaco
Malta
Greece
Morocco
Tunisia
Algeria
Libya
Former Spanish Sahara
Mauritania
Mali
Niger
Chad
Sudan
Senegal
Burkina Faso
Benin
Nigeria
Guinea
Sierra Leone
Côte d'Ivoire
Ghana
Liberia
Togo
Equatorial Guinea
São Tomé and Príncipe
Gabon
Congo
Cameroon
Central African Republic
Dem.Rep.of Congo
Rwanda
Burundi
Uganda
Kenya
Tanzania
Angola
Zambia
Malawi
Mozambique
Namibia
Zimbabwe
Botswana
South Africa
Swaziland
Lesotho
Madagascar
Comoros
Mayotte (Fr)
Seychelles
Mauritius
Réunion (Fr)

Estonia
Latvia
Russian Fed.
Lithuania
Belarus
Poland
Ukraine
Moldova
Romania
Bulgaria
Georgia
Armenia
Azer-baijan
Turkey
Cyprus
Lebanon
Syrian Arab Rep.
Israel
West Bank and Gaza
Jordan
Iraq
Islamic Rep. of Iran
Kuwait
Bahrain
Qatar
Saudi Arabia
Arab Rep. of Egypt
United Arab Emirates
Oman
Rep. of Yemen
Eritrea
Djibouti
Ethiopia
Somalia

Russian Federation
Kazakhstan
Uzbekistan
Turkmenistan
Kyrgyz Rep.
Tajikistan
Afghanistan
Pakistan
India
Nepal
Bhutan
Bangladesh
Myanmar
Mongolia
China
Dem.People's Rep.of Korea
Rep.of Korea
Japan
Macao (Port)
Lao P.D.R.
Thailand
Vietnam
Cambodia
Philippines
Malaysia
Brunei
Singapore
Indonesia
Sri Lanka
Maldives

N. Mariana Islands (US)
Guam (US)
Federated States of Micronesia
Palau
Marshall Islands
Nauru
Kiribati
Papua New Guinea
Solomon Islands
Tuvalu
Vanuatu
Fiji
New Caledonia (Fr)
Australia
New Zealand

Antarctica

IBRD 29206

Germany
Poland
Czech Republic
Ukraine
Slovak Republic
Austria
Hungary
Slovenia
Romania
Croatia
Bosnia and Herzegovina
Fed. Rep. of Yugoslavia (Serb./Mont.)
San Marino
Bulgaria
Italy
FYR Macedonia
Albania
Greece

CONTENTS

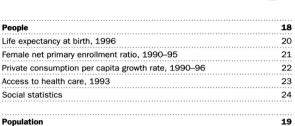

ECONOMY

STATES AND MARKETS

GLOBAL LINKS

Introduction

This 30th *World Bank Atlas* has been expanded to incorporate more of the topics covered by its companion volume, the *World Development Indicators*, and is a third longer to reflect new design features and changes in content.

Last year's *Atlas* had separate sections on People, Environment, Economy, and States and Markets. This year's adds two new sections: World View, which focuses on development goals for the 21st century, and Global Links, which explores issues of global economic integration such as trade, financial flows, aid, and migration.

The *Atlas* retains its primary strength of providing readers with a quick view of the state of life on our planet, measured by a range of key development indicators and illustrated by colorful and informative maps. Every effort has been made to standardize the data and to observe international definitions and classifications, but differences in statistical and collection methods mean that the indicators are not always strictly comparable. The quality of the data also remains a major issue. As in earlier editions, brief descriptions of the data are included in the technical notes. More detailed notes are available in the *World Development Indicators* and in its CD-ROM edition, which also includes 30-year time series.

Introduction

Ce 30e *World Bank Atlas* a été élargie de manière à couvrir un plus grand nombre de sujets parmi ceux inclus dans *World Development Indicators,* l'autre publication de la Banque mondiale qui lui fait pendant. Avec une maquette et un contenu totalement remaniés, elle a été amplifiée du tiers par rapport à l'édition précédente.

L'*Atlas* de l'année dernière comprenait quatre sections : Population, Environnement, Économie, État et Marché. Celui-ci en compte deux de plus : Perspective Mondiale, centrée sur les objectifs du développement à l'horizon du XXIe siècle ; et Interactions Économiques Mondiales, consacrée aux questions soulevées par la mondialisation de l'économie (en matière d'échanges, de flux financiers, d'aide et de migrations, par exemple).

Mais l'aspect qui fait avant tout la force de cet *Atlas* reste le même : il vise à donner au lecteur un aperçu de la situation des êtres humains sur notre planète en prenant pour référence une série d'indicateurs de développement clés, et en synthétisant cette information au moyen de cartes en couleurs. Bien qu'on se soit efforcé de normaliser les données et de respecter les définitions et classifications internationales, les différences de méthodes statistiques et de modes de collecte des données font que les indicateurs ne sont pas toujours strictement comparables. La qualité des données demeure aussi un problème majeur. Comme dans les éditions antérieures, une brève description des données est fournie dans les notes techniques. Des notes plus détaillées figurent dans *World Development Indicators* et dans la version CD-ROM de cet ouvrage, qui comporte aussi des séries chronologiques sur 30 ans.

Introducción

Esta trigésima edición del *World Bank Atlas* se ha ampliado a fin de incorporar un mayor número de los temas abordados en *World Development Indicators,* el volumen complementario del *Atlas.* Además, la presente edición es un tercio más larga que la anterior puesto que en ella se incluyen algunas características de diseño novedosas y modificaciones en su contenido.

En el *Atlas* del año pasado había secciones separadas sobre Población, Medio Ambiente, Economía, y Estados y Mercados. Este año se han agregado dos nuevas secciones: Perspectiva Mundial, centrada en los objetivos de desarrollo para el siglo XXI, e Integración Mundial, en la que se examinan algunos aspectos de la integración económica mundial como el comercio, los flujos financieros, la asistencia, y las migraciones.

El *Atlas* mantiene su principal ventaja, la de proporcionar a sus lectores un panorama sucinto de las condiciones de vida en nuestro planeta, medidas por un conjunto de indicadores fundamentales del desarrollo, e ilustradas con mapas a todo color. No se han escatimado esfuerzos para uniformar y observar las definiciones y clasificaciones internacionales, pero dadas las diferencias que existen en los métodos estadísticos y de recopilación de datos, los indicadores no son siempre estrictamente comparables. Además, la calidad de los datos sigue constituyendo un problema importante. Como en ediciones anteriores, en las notas técnicas se incluyen breves descripciones de los datos presentados. En *World Development Indicators* y su versión en CD-ROM, que también incluye series cronológicas de 30 años, se presentan más notas pormenorizadas.

World View

Living standards have risen dramatically over the past 25 years. Despite an increase in population from 2.9 billion people in 1970 to 4.8 billion in 1996, per capita income growth in developing countries averaged more than 1.4 percent a year. Although the number of people living in poverty continues to grow, millions have had lifted from them the yoke of poverty and despair. As a result the proportion of the poor is holding steady at less than a third of the developing world's population.

Growth in average incomes has brought substantial improvements in social indicators. Infant mortality rates have fallen from 104 per 1,000 live births in 1970–75 to 59 per 1,000 in 1996. On average, life expectancy has risen by four months a year since 1970. Growth in food production has substantially outpaced that of population. Primary school enrollments continue to rise. Gender disparities have narrowed, with the ratio of girls to boys in secondary schools rising on average from 70 to 100 in 1980 to 82 to 100 in 1993. And adult literacy has increased, from 46 to 70 percent. The developing world today is healthier, wealthier, better fed, and better educated.

But progress has been far from even. Take mortality. All developing regions have seen infant and child mortality decline sharply. But South Asia's infant mortality rates today are about the same as East Asia's in the early 1970s, reflecting poor progress in South Asia and favorable initial social conditions in East Asia. Similarly, Sub-Saharan Africa's infant mortality rates are well above those in East Asia some 25 years ago. On average, 132 of every 1,000 African children die before the age of 5, and 91 of 1,000 die before the age of 1.

D VIEW

Perspective Mondiale

Les niveaux de vie ont progressé en 25 ans d'une manière spectaculaire. Alors que la population passait de 2,9 milliards en 1970 à 4,8 milliards en 1996, l'augmentation moyenne du revenu par habitant dans les pays en développement a dépassé 1,4 % par an. Certes, le nombre d'individus vivant dans la pauvreté continue de croître, mais des millions d'êtres humains ont déjà échappé au joug de la misère, de sorte que la proportion de pauvres dans le monde reste à moins du tiers de la population.

La progression des revenus moyens s'est accompagnée d'une nette amélioration des indicateurs sociaux. Les taux de mortalité infantile sont tombés de 104 pour 1 000 naissances vivantes pour la période 1970–75 à 59 pour 1 000 en 1996. L'espérance de vie à la naissance a augmenté en moyenne de quatre mois par an depuis 1970. L'augmentation de la production alimentaire a été sensiblement supérieure à la croissance démographique. Les taux de scolarisation primaire continuent d'augmenter. Les disparités entre les sexes ont diminué, puisque la proportion filles-garçons dans l'enseignement secondaire est passée de 70 pour 100 en 1980 à 82 pour 100 en 1993. Enfin, le taux d'alphabétisation des adultes a progressé de 46 à 70 %. Les habitants du monde en développement sont aujourd'hui en meilleure santé, plus riches, mieux nourris et mieux éduqués.

Mais le progrès n'a pas été uniforme, loin de là. Exemple : la mortalité. Toutes les régions en développement ont vu la mortalité infantile et juvénile chuter fortement. Mais les taux de mortalité infantile de l'Asie du Sud sont aujourd'hui à peu près au niveau où étaient ceux de l'Asie de l'Est au début des années 70, ce qui témoigne à la fois d'un manque de progrès en Asie du Sud et d'une situation sociale initiale favorable en Asie de l'Est. De même, les taux de mortalité infantile de l'Afrique subsaharienne sont bien supérieurs à ceux de l'Asie de l'Est il y a environ 25 ans. En moyenne, 132 enfants africains sur 1 000 meurent avant l'âge de 5 ans, et 91 sur 1 000 meurent avant 1 an.

Perspective Mundial

En los últimos 25 años se ha producido un espectacular aumento de los niveles de vida. Pese a que el número de habitantes subió de 2.900 millones en 1970 a 4.800 millones en 1996, el ingreso medio per cápita de los países en desarrollo aumentó más de un 1,4% anual. Aunque las personas que viven en la pobreza son cada vez más, se ha logrado liberar a millones de ellas del yugo de la miseria y de la desesperación. En consecuencia, la proporción de pobres se mantiene constante en un nivel equivalente a menos de un tercio de la población total del mundo en desarrollo.

El aumento del ingreso medio se ha traducido en una notable mejora de los indicadores sociales. Las tasas de mortalidad infantil han bajado de 104 por cada 1.000 nacidos vivos en 1970–75 a 59 por 1.000 en 1996. La esperanza de vida media ha aumentado cuatro meses al año desde 1970. El incremento de la producción de alimentos ha sido notablemente más rápido que el crecimiento demográfico. La matriculación en escuelas primarias sigue en aumento. Se han reducido las disparidades por razón de género, y la proporción de niñas con respecto al número de niños en las escuelas secundarias ha subido en promedio de 70 por cada 100 en 1980 a 82 por cada 100 en 1993. La tasa de alfabetización también ha subido, habiendo pasado del 46% al 70%. Hoy en día, los países en desarrollo registran niveles más altos de salud, riqueza, y educación, y están mejor alimentados.

Con todo, estos avances distan mucho de ser homogéneos. Veamos, por ejemplo, las tasas de mortalidad. En todas las regiones del mundo en desarrollo se ha producido un acusado descenso de las tasas de mortalidad de niños y lactantes. No obstante, en Asia meridional las tasas de mortalidad infantil siguen siendo más o menos las mismas de Asia oriental a principios de los años setenta, debido a la lentitud de los progresos en la primera y a las favorables condiciones de partida de la segunda. De la misma manera, las tasas de mortalidad infantil de África al sur del Sahara son mucho más altas que las de Asia oriental hace unos 25 años. En promedio, 132 de cada 1.000 niños mueren en África antes de los cinco años, y 91 de cada 1.000 antes de cumplir un año.

International Development Goals

Recent United Nations conferences have adopted several goals for the 21st century, and members of the OECD's Development Assistance Committee have pledged to support developing countries who are committed to achieving the following six:
- Reducing by half the proportion of people living in extreme poverty by 2015.
- Achieving universal primary education in all countries by 2015.
- Demonstrating progress toward gender equality and the empowerment of women by eliminating gender disparities in primary and secondary education by 2005.
- Reducing by two-thirds infant and child mortality rates and by three-quarters maternal mortality rates by 2015.
- Providing access to reproductive health services for all individuals of appropriate age by no later than 2015.
- Implementing national strategies for sustainable development by 2005 to ensure that the current loss of environmental resources is reversed globally and nationally by 2015.

Such commitments are too often received with cynicism. After all, the world's poor are testament to the past lack of political will to achieve such goals. Can we make it different this time?

Perhaps, because new forces are at work. First, there is a new consensus on development. Gone with the Cold War are sterile, ideological debates over the roles of the state and market. In their place is a more pragmatic approach to effective and broad-based development strategies. Second, the achievements of some developing countries show that the worst forms of poverty can be undone, and that investments in human capital and the poor can have high economic returns.

Objectifs de Développement au Plan International

Les conférences récemment tenues sous les auspices des Nations Unies ont vu l'adoption de plusieurs objectifs pour le XXIe siècle, et les membres du Comité d'aide au développement de l'OCDE se sont engagés à soutenir les pays en développement qui sont déterminés à réaliser les six suivants :
- Réduire de moitié, d'ici 2015, la proportion d'individus vivant dans une extrême pauvreté.
- Assurer l'enseignement primaire universel dans tous les pays d'ici 2015.
- Faire des progrès tangibles sur la voie de l'égalité des sexes et de l'émancipation des femmes grâce à l'élimination des disparités entre filles et garçons dans l'enseignement primaire et secondaire d'ici 2005.
- Réduire les taux de mortalité infantile et juvénile des deux tiers et les taux de mortalité maternelle des trois quarts d'ici 2015.
- Assurer l'accès aux services de santé génésique pour tous les individus d'âge voulu en 2015 au plus tard.
- Mettre en oeuvre des stratégies nationales pour un développement durable d'ici 2005, pour faire en sorte que la tendance actuelle à la perte des ressources environnementales s'inverse à l'échelon national et planétaire d'ici 2015.

Les engagements de ce type sont trop souvent accueillis avec cynisme. Après tout, les individus qui vivent encore dans la pauvreté de par le monde témoignent du fait que les pays ont jusqu'ici manqué de la volonté politique nécessaire pour atteindre ces buts. Peut-on faire en sorte qu'il en aille autrement cette fois-ci ?

Peut-être, car une dynamique nouvelle s'est instaurée. D'une part, la question du développement fait désormais l'objet d'un consensus. La fin de la guerre froide a également marqué la fin des débats idéologiques stériles sur le rôle de l'État et du marché. Ils ont fait place à une approche plus pragmatique pour l'établissement de stratégies de développement efficaces et diversifiées. D'autre part, les succès obtenus par certains pays en développement montrent que la pauvreté sous ses pires formes peut être éliminée, et que les investissements dans le capital humain et dans les pauvres peuvent être très rentables du point de vue économique.

Metas de Desarrollo a Nivel Internacional

Algunas conferencias recientes de las Naciones Unidas han adoptado varias metas para el siglo XXI, y los miembros del Comité de Asistencia para el Desarrollo, de la OCDE, han prometido ayudar a los países en desarrollo que se comprometan con los seis objetivos siguientes:
- Reducir a la mitad la proporción de personas que viven en situación de extrema pobreza para el año 2015.
- Lograr la cobertura universal de la educación primaria en todos los países para el año 2015.
- Demostrar que se ha avanzado en materia de igualdad de géneros y promoción de la autonomía de la mujer eliminando las disparidades por razón de género en la educación primaria y secundaria para el año 2005.
- Reducir en dos tercios las tasas de mortalidad de lactantes y niños menores de cinco años, y en tres cuartos las tasas de mortalidad materna para el año 2015.
- Facilitar el acceso a los servicios de salud reproductiva a todos los individuos de edad apropiada, a más tardar, para el año 2015.
- Poner en marcha estrategias nacionales de desarrollo sostenible para el año 2005, a fin de invertir a escala mundial y nacional la actual tendencia de pérdida de recursos ambientales para el año 2015.
- Sin embargo, con harta frecuencia este tipo de compromisos se reciben con cinismo. Después de todo, la pobreza del mundo es el legado de una falta de voluntad política en el pasado para ponerlos por obra. ¿Podremos actuar de forma diferente esta vez?

Quizás sí, porque ahora se da una conjunción de nuevos factores. En primer lugar, existe un nuevo consenso en torno al desarrollo. Junto con la guerra fría han desaparecido los debates estériles sobre el papel que deben desempeñar el Estado y el mercado. En su lugar, se ha adoptado un enfoque más pragmático para instrumentar estrategias de desarrollo eficaces y diversificadas. En segundo lugar, los logros conseguidos por algunos países en desarrollo demuestran que incluso en las peores situaciones de pobreza se puede desandar el camino equivocado, y que las inversiones en capital humano y en la promoción de los sectores pobres pueden producir una elevada rentabilidad económica.

The international community has set ambitious goals for itself in the next century: reducing poverty, closing large gaps in social development, and protecting the environment.

Goals for social development

Primary education
Achieving universal primary education in all countries by 2015

Gender equality in education
Demonstrating progress toward gender equality and the empowerment of women by eliminating gender disparities in primary and secondary education by 2005

Infant, child, and maternal mortality
Reducing by two-thirds the mortality rates for infants and children under five and by three-fourths the mortality rates for mothers by 2015

Infant mortality
↓ 2/3

Maternal mortality
↓ 3/4

Reproductive health
Providing access to reproductive health services for all individuals of appropriate age no later than 2015

Goals for economic well-being

Poverty
Reducing by half the proportion of people in extreme poverty by 2015

↓ 1/2

Environment
Implementing national strategies for sustainable development by 2005 to ensure that the current loss of environmental resources is reversed globally and nationally by 2015

Goals for environmental sustainability and regeneration

Meeting these goals will not be easy. It will require a strong commitment by developing countries, a renewed effort by international development agencies, and considerable support from advanced countries.

How far do we have to go?

Goal: reduce number in poverty by half

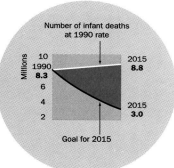

Growth of poverty at current rates

Billions of poor

3
2
1993 **1.3**
1987 **1.2**
2015 **1.9**
2015 **0.9**

Goal for 2015

Goal: reduce infant deaths by two-thirds

Number of infant deaths at 1990 rate

Millions

10
1990 **8.3**
6
4
2
2015 **8.8**
2015 **3.0**

Goal for 2015

Goal: reduce under-five deaths by two-thirds

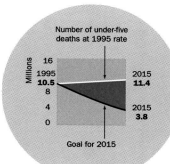

Number of under-five deaths at 1995 rate

Millions

16
1995 **10.5**
8
4
0
2015 **11.4**
2015 **3.8**

Goal for 2015

Goal: achieve universal primary education

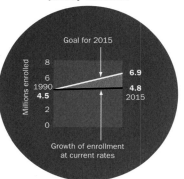

Goal for 2015

Millions enrolled

8
6
1990 **4.5**
2
0
6.9
4.8 2015

Growth of enrollment at current rates

Income growth in the 1990s has slowed the increase in world poverty. But continuing population growth and unequal distributions of income leave many people vulnerable to extreme poverty.

Asia contains more than half of the world's people. But the populations of Africa and the Middle East are growing fa

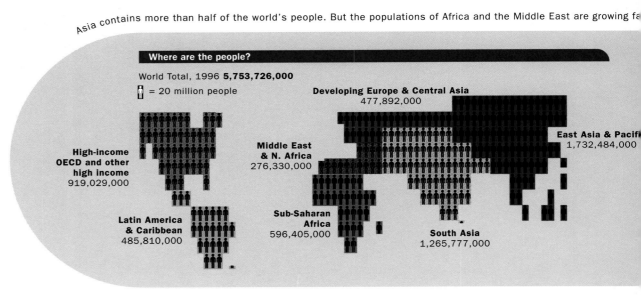

Where are the people?

World Total, 1996 **5,753,726,000**

👤 = 20 million people

Developing Europe & Central Asia
477,892,000

High-income OECD and other high income
919,029,000

Middle East & N. Africa
276,330,000

East Asia & Pacifi
1,732,484,000

Latin America & Caribbean
485,810,000

Sub-Saharan Africa
596,405,000

South Asia
1,265,777,000

80% of the world's output is produced in high-income economies—which contain only 16% of the world's

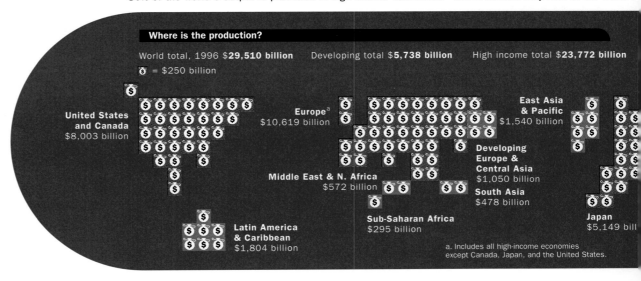

Where is the production?

World total, 1996 **$29,510 billion**   Developing total **$5,738 billion**   High income total **$23,772 billion**

💲 = $250 billion

United States and Canada
$8,003 billion

Europe[a]
$10,619 billion

East Asia & Pacific
$1,540 billion

Developing Europe & Central Asia
$1,050 billion

Middle East & N. Africa
$572 billion

South Asia
$478 billion

Latin America & Caribbean
$1,804 billion

Sub-Saharan Africa
$295 billion

Japan
$5,149 bill

a. Includes all high-income economies except Canada, Japan, and the United States.

Measured by the common standard of $1 a day, 1.3 billion people in the developing world live in extreme poverty. Most of these people are in Asia.

Many countries will be able to reduce poverty if they can sustain recent growth rates and avoid worsening income distribution. Others will need to grow much faster.

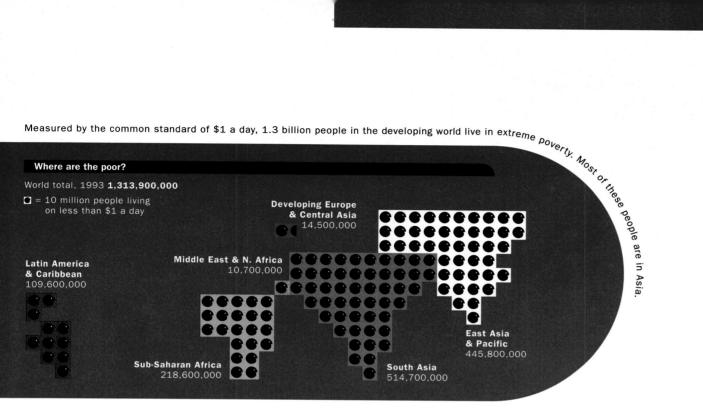

Where are the poor?

World total, 1993 **1,313,900,000**

▢ = 10 million people living on less than $1 a day

Developing Europe & Central Asia
14,500,000

Latin America & Caribbean
109,600,000

Middle East & N. Africa
10,700,000

East Asia & Pacific
445,800,000

Sub-Saharan Africa
218,600,000

South Asia
514,700,000

80% of the world's poor live in 12 countries—and 62% live in China and India.

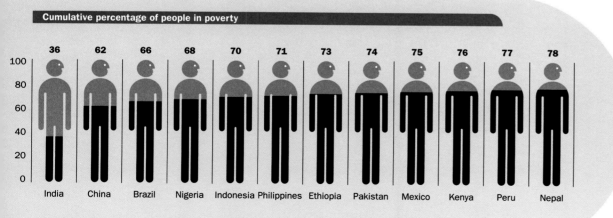

Cumulative percentage of people in poverty

	36	62	66	68	70	71	73	74	75	76	77	78
	India	China	Brazil	Nigeria	Indonesia	Philippines	Ethiopia	Pakistan	Mexico	Kenya	Peru	Nepal

Note: The figure shows countries with more than 10 million people in poverty and for which comparable data are available. Data for Bangladesh and the Democratic Republic of Congo are not available, but they are included in world estimates.

GNP per capita is one measure of average welfare. To make comparisons across countries, national currencies must be converted to a common unit. The World Bank Atlas method uses official or market exchange rates. The purchasing power parity (PPP) method uses international comparisons of average price levels. Only economies with 1996 estimates are included.

Rankings of economies based on GNP per capita

Rank	GNP per capita, 1996 World Bank Atlas method	$	Rank	GNP per capita, 1996 purchasing power parity method	$	Rank	GNP per capita, 1996 World Bank Atlas method	$	Rank	GNP per capita, 1996 purchasing power parity method	$
1	Luxembourg	45,360	1	Luxembourg	34,480	41	Croatia	3,800	41	Mauritius	9,000
2	Switzerland	44,350	2	United States	28,020	42	Mauritius	3,710	42	Oman	8,680
3	Japan	40,940	3	Singapore	26,910	43	Mexico	3,670	43	Antigua and Barbuda	8,660
4	Norway	34,510	4	Switzerland	26,340	44	South Africa	3,520	44	Venezuela	8,130
5	Denmark	32,100	5	Hong Kong, China[a]	24,260	45	St. Lucia	3,500	45	Uruguay	7,760
6	Singapore	30,550	6	Japan	23,420	46	Slovak Republic	3,410	46	Mexico	7,660
7	Germany	28,870	7	Norway	23,220	47	Poland	3,230	47	Slovak Republic	7,460
8	Austria	28,110	8	Belgium	22,390	48	Dominica	3,090	48	South Africa	7,450
9	United States	28,020	9	Denmark	22,120	49	Estonia	3,080	49	Botswana	7,390
10	Iceland	26,580	10	Iceland	21,710	50	Panama	3,080	50	St. Kitts and Nevis	7,310
11	Belgium	26,440	11	Austria	21,650	51	Venezuela	3,020	51	Panama	7,060
12	France	26,270	12	France	21,510	52	Lebanon	2,970	52	Hungary	6,730
13	Netherlands	25,940	13	Canada	21,380	53	Thailand	2,960	53	Colombia	6,720
14	Sweden	25,710	14	Germany	21,110	54	Grenada	2,880	54	Thailand	6,700
15	Hong Kong, China[a]	24,290	15	Netherlands	20,850	55	Turkey	2,830	55	Costa Rica	6,470
16	Finland	23,240	16	Cyprus	20,490	56	Belize	2,700	56	Brazil	6,340
17	Australia	20,090	17	United Kingdom	19,960	57	Costa Rica	2,640	57	Gabon	6,300
18	Italy	19,880	18	Italy	19,890	58	Fiji	2,470	58	Trinidad and Tobago	6,100
19	United Kingdom	19,600	19	Australia	19,870	59	Peru	2,420	59	Lebanon	6,060
20	Canada	19,020	20	Sweden	18,770	60	Russian Federation	2,410	60	Turkey	6,060
21	Ireland	17,110	21	Finland	18,260	61	St. Vincent/Grenadines	2,370	61	Poland	6,000
22	Israel	15,870	22	Israel	18,100	62	Latvia	2,300	62	Namibia	5,390
23	New Zealand	15,720	23	United Arab Emirates	17,000	63	Lithuania	2,280	63	Iran, Islamic Rep.	5,360
24	Spain	14,350	24	Ireland	16,750	64	Namibia	2,250	64	St. Lucia	4,920
25	Greece	11,460	25	New Zealand	16,500	65	Colombia	2,140	65	Ecuador	4,730
26	Korea, Rep.	10,610	26	Qatar	16,330	66	Belarus	2,070	66	Estonia	4,660
27	Portugal	10,160	27	Spain	15,290	67	Micronesia, Fed. Sts.	2,070	67	Algeria	4,620
28	Slovenia	9,240	28	Bahrain	13,970	68	Tunisia	1,930	68	Romania	4,580
29	Argentina	8,380	29	Malta	13,870	69	Marshall Islands	1,890	69	Tunisia	4,550
30	Antigua and Barbuda	7,330	30	Portugal	13,450	70	Paraguay	1,850	70	Peru	4,410
31	Seychelles	6,850	31	Korea, Rep.	13,080	71	Tonga	1,790	71	Dominica	4,390
32	St. Kitts and Nevis	5,870	32	Greece	12,730	72	El Salvador	1,700	72	Dominican Republic	4,390
33	Uruguay	5,760	33	Slovenia	12,110	73	Jordan	1,650	73	Lithuania	4,390
34	Chile	4,860	34	Chile	11,700	74	Dominican Republic	1,600	74	Belarus	4,380
35	Czech Republic	4,740	35	Czech Republic	10,870	75	Jamaica	1,600	75	Grenada	4,340
36	Brazil	4,400	36	Barbados	10,510	76	Romania	1,600	76	Croatia	4,290
37	Malaysia	4,370	37	Malaysia	10,390	77	Algeria	1,520	77	Bulgaria	4,280
38	Hungary	4,340	38	Bahamas, The	10,180	78	Ecuador	1,500	78	Russian Federation	4,190
39	Gabon	3,950	39	Saudi Arabia	9,700	79	Guatemala	1,470	79	Belize	4,170
40	Trinidad and Tobago	3,870	40	Argentina	9,530	80	Kazakhstan	1,350	80	St. Vincent/Grenadines	4,160

Rank	GNP per capita, 1996 World Bank Atlas method	$	Rank	GNP per capita, 1996 purchasing power parity method	$
81	Morocco	1,290	81	Fiji	4,070
82	Vanuatu	1,290	82	Guatemala	3,820
83	Swaziland	1,210	83	Latvia	3,650
84	Ukraine	1,200	84	Jordan	3,570
85	Bulgaria	1,190	85	Philippines	3,550
86	Samoa	1,170	86	Paraguay	3,480
87	Philippines	1,160	87	Jamaica	3,450
88	Syrian Arab Republic	1,160	88	China	3,330
89	Papua New Guinea	1,150	89	Morocco	3,320
90	Egypt, Arab Rep.	1,080	90	Swaziland	3,320
91	Indonesia	1,080	91	Indonesia	3,310
92	Maldives	1,080	92	Kazakhstan	3,230
93	Cape Verde	1,010	93	Maldives	3,140
94	Uzbekistan	1,010	94	Syrian Arab Republic	3,020
95	Suriname	1,000	95	Vanuatu	3,020
96	Macedonia, FYR	990	96	Bolivia	2,860
97	Turkmenistan	940	97	Egypt, Arab Rep.	2,860
98	Kiribati	920	98	Papua New Guinea	2,820
99	Solomon Islands	900	99	El Salvador	2,790
100	Georgia	850	100	Equatorial Guinea	2,690
101	Bolivia	830	101	Cape Verde	2,640
102	Albania	820	102	Suriname	2,630
103	China	750	103	Uzbekistan	2,450
104	Sri Lanka	740	104	Lesotho	2,380
105	Guyana	690	105	Sri Lanka	2,290
106	Congo, Rep.	670	106	Guyana	2,280
107	Côte d'Ivoire	660	107	Solomon Islands	2,250
108	Honduras	660	108	Ukraine	2,230
109	Lesotho	660	109	Zimbabwe	2,200
110	Armenia	630	110	Armenia	2,160
111	Cameroon	610	111	Honduras	2,130
112	Zimbabwe	610	112	Turkmenistan	2,010
113	Moldova	590	113	Kyrgyz Republic	1,970
114	Senegal	570	114	Mongolia	1,820
115	Guinea	560	115	Georgia	1,810
116	Kyrgyz Republic	550	116	Mauritania	1,810
117	Equatorial Guinea	530	117	Ghana	1,790
118	Azerbaijan	480	118	Comoros	1,770
119	Pakistan	480	119	Cameroon	1,760
120	Mauritania	470	120	Nicaragua	1,760

Rank	GNP per capita, 1996 World Bank Atlas method	$	Rank	GNP per capita, 1996 purchasing power parity method	$
121	Comoros	450	121	Guinea	1,720
122	Lao PDR	400	122	Senegal	1,650
123	Bhutan	390	123	Togo	1,650
124	India	380	124	Pakistan	1,600
125	Nicaragua	380	125	Côte d'Ivoire	1,580
126	Yemen, Rep.	380	126	India	1,580
127	Ghana	360	127	Vietnam	1,570
128	Mongolia	360	128	Azerbaijan	1,490
129	Zambia	360	129	Moldova	1,440
130	Benin	350	130	Central African Republic	1,430
131	Tajikistan	340	131	Congo, Rep.	1,410
132	São Tomé and Principe	330	132	Gambia, The	1,280
133	Kenya	320	133	Lao PDR	1,250
134	Central African Republic	310	134	Benin	1,230
135	Haiti	310	135	Haiti	1,130
136	Cambodia	300	136	Kenya	1,130
137	Togo	300	137	Nepal	1,090
138	Uganda	300	138	Angola	1,030
139	Vietnam	290	139	Guinea-Bissau	1,030
140	Angola	270	140	Uganda	1,030
141	Bangladesh	260	141	Bangladesh	1,010
142	Guinea-Bissau	250	142	Burkina Faso	950
143	Madagascar	250	143	Niger	920
144	Mali	240	144	Madagascar	900
145	Nigeria	240	145	Tajikistan	900
146	Burkina Faso	230	146	Chad	880
147	Nepal	210	147	Nigeria	870
148	Niger	200	148	Zambia	860
149	Sierra Leone	200	149	Congo, Dem. Rep.	790
150	Rwanda	190	150	Yemen, Rep.	790
151	Malawi	180	151	Mali	710
152	Burundi	170	152	Malawi	690
153	Tanzania	170	153	Rwanda	630
154	Chad	160	154	Burundi	590
155	Congo, Dem. Rep.	130	155	Sierra Leone	510
156	Ethiopia	100	156	Ethiopia	500
157	Mozambique	80	157	Mozambique	500

Note: See the *Economy* table (pages 42–43) for country notes.
a. Data for GNP are for GDP.

Comparisons of GNP using official exchange rates tend to undervalue low- and middle-income economies with relatively low prices. The GNP per capita of China, for example, is less than 3 percent of that of the United States when measured at official rates. But it rises to almost 12 percent when measured using PPPs. Services are often the most undervalued component of GNP in low- and middle-income economies.

People

Development is about people and their well-being—about people developing their capabilities to provide for their families, to act as stewards of the environment, to form civil societies that are just and orderly. Human capital development—the result of education and improvements in health and nutrition—is both an end and a means to achieving social progress.

Human capital is crucial to raising the living standards of the poor. Health care and good nutrition reduce sickness and mortality and improve labor productivity. Literacy and numeracy broaden horizons, making it easier for people to learn new skills throughout their working lives, and thus ensure full participation in social and economic life. By raising people's productivity, investments in education stimulate growth.

Better education and health enable couples to make more informed decisions about the number and spacing of their children and about their schooling, and to safeguard maternal and child health. The improved health of educated people motivates them to make still more investments in their education and health. The relationship between investments and outcomes is thus mutually reinforcing, justifying investments in human capital on both economic and equity grounds.

Because the poor's most significant asset is their labor, the most effective way to improve their welfare is to increase their employment opportunities and labor productivity through investments in human capital. The poor are often unable to finance such investments. Thus the challenge is to create an enabling environment and to mobilize resources for human capital investments.

Population

L'objet du développement est l'individu et son bien-être : il s'agit de donner aux gens les moyens de pourvoir aux besoins de leur famille, d'assurer une gestion avisée de l'environnement et de constituer des sociétés où règnent l'ordre et la justice. En matière de progrès social, la valorisation du capital humain rendue possible par l'éducation et l'amélioration des niveaux de santé et de nutrition est à la fois une fin et un moyen.

Le capital humain est déterminant pour l'amélioration du niveau de vie des pauvres. Les soins de santé et une nutrition appropriée réduisent les maladies et la mortalité, et améliorent la productivité de la main-d'oeuvre. Le fait pour une personne de savoir lire, écrire et compter élargit ses horizons ; il lui permet d'acquérir plus facilement des compétences nouvelles tout au long de sa vie professionnelle, et de participer ainsi pleinement à la vie économique et sociale de son pays. En améliorant la productivité des individus, les investissements dans l'éducation favorisent la croissance.

Un meilleur niveau d'éducation et de santé permet aux couples de décider en meilleure connaissance de cause du nombre d'enfants qu'ils veulent avoir, de leur espacement et de leur instruction, et de préserver la santé maternelle et infantile. Et pour des individus éduqués, une meilleure santé est un élément qui incite à investir encore davantage dans leur éducation et leur santé. Les liens entre les investissements et leurs effets se renforcent ainsi mutuellement, justifiant l'investissement dans le capital humain à la fois pour des raisons d'équité et sur la base de critères économiques.

Comme leur force de travail est le principal atout des pauvres, la meilleure façon d'améliorer leur niveau de vie consiste à améliorer leurs possibilités d'emploi et leur productivité par des investissements dans le capital humain. Dans bien des cas, les pauvres ne sont pas en mesure de financer de tels investissements, et le problème consiste donc à établir un milieu propice et à mobiliser des ressources pour les investissements dans ce domaine.

Población

El desarrollo se centra en las personas y en su bienestar —en el fortalecimiento de su capacidad para mantener a sus familias, proteger el medio ambiente y formar sociedades civiles que vivan en la justicia y el orden. El perfeccionamiento del capital humano —resultado de la educación y de las mejoras en los campos de la salud y la nutrición— es a la vez un fin y un medio para conseguir el progreso social.

El capital humano es esencial para elevar el nivel de vida de los pobres. La atención de la salud y una buena nutrición reducen los índices de enfermedad y mortalidad y aumentan la productividad laboral. La alfabetización y los conocimientos básicos de aritmética abren nuevos horizontes, facilitan el aprendizaje de nuevas materias a lo largo de la vida laboral, y garantizan una plena participación en la vida económica y social. Al elevar la productividad de las personas, la inversión en educación estimula el crecimiento.

Una mejor educación y un mejor estado de salud permiten a las parejas tomar decisiones más informadas con respecto al espaciamiento de los nacimientos y al número de hijos, así como a la educación de éstos, además de proteger la salud maternoinfantil. Cuando la población, además de disfrutar de un nivel de educación más alto, es más sana, tiene más motivación para seguir invirtiendo en su educación y su salud. Así pues, existe una correlación entre las inversiones y los resultados, que justifica la inversión en capital humano tanto por motivos económicos como por razones de equidad.

Como el activo más importante con que cuentan los pobres es su trabajo, la forma más eficaz de aumentar sus niveles de bienestar es incrementar sus posibilidades de empleo y su productividad laboral a través de inversiones en capital humano. Con frecuencia, los pobres carecen de medios para financiar estas inversiones. Así pues, el desafío está en crear un entorno propicio y en movilizar recursos para invertir en capital humano.

Life expectancy at birth, 1996

The average number of years a newborn baby would live if patterns of mortality prevailing for all people at the time of its birth were to stay the same throughout its life.

Espérance de vie à la naissance, 1996

Nombre moyen d'années que vivrait un nouveau-né si les tendances de la mortalité observées pour l'ensemble de la population au moment de sa naissance restaient inchangées tout au long de son existence.

Esperanza de vida al nacer, 1996

Número de años que viviría un recién nacido, en promedio, si las tendencias de mortalidad de toda la población en el momento de su nacimiento se mantuvieran constantes durante toda su vida.

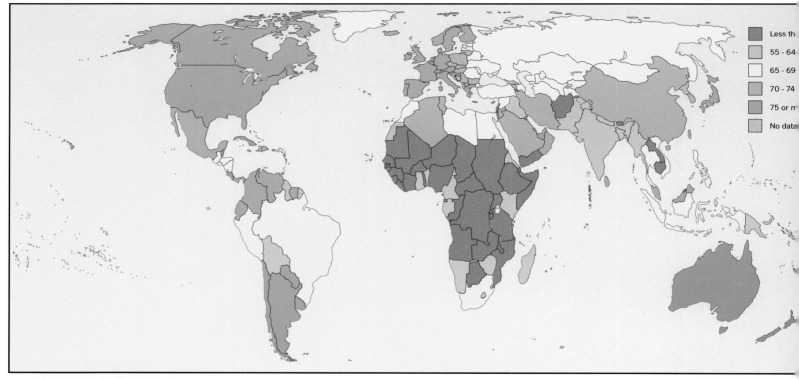

Less th
55 - 64
65 - 69
70 - 74
75 or m
No data

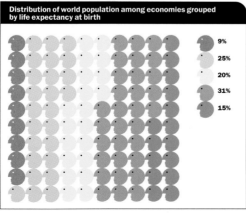

Distribution of world population among economies grouped by life expectancy at birth

9%
25%
20%
31%
15%

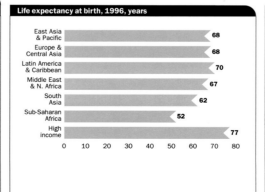

Life expectancy at birth, 1996, years

East Asia & Pacific	68
Europe & Central Asia	68
Latin America & Caribbean	70
Middle East & N. Africa	67
South Asia	62
Sub-Saharan Africa	52
High income	77

0 10 20 30 40 50 60 70 80

Life expectancy at birth, 1996, years

	Economies	GNP $ millions 1996	Population millions 1996	GNP per capita $ 1996
Less than 55	36	126,855	514	250
55–64	28	604,698	1,432	420
65–69	34	2,307,991	1,129	2,040
70–74	50	3,056,869	1,766	1,730
75 or more	47	23,395,280	905	25,840
No data	15	17,922	8	2,360

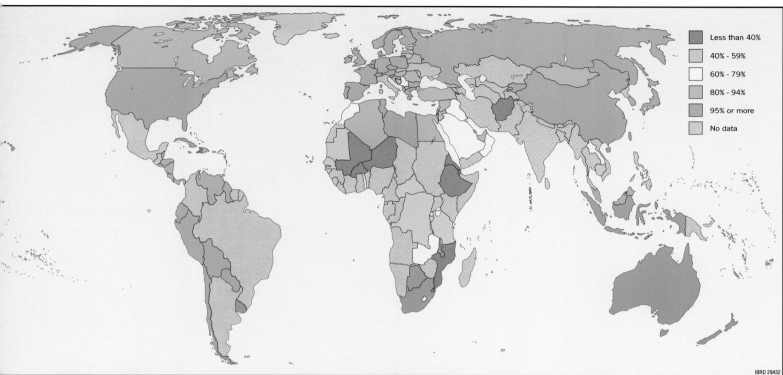

Less than 40%

40% - 59%

60% - 79%

80% - 94%

95% or more

No data

IBRD 29432

The ratio of the number of girls of official school age enrolled in primary school to the number of official school-age girls in the population.

Taux net de scolarisation primaire féminine, 1990–95
Pourcentage des filles d'âge scolaire inscrites à l'école primaire.

Porcentaje neto de matrícula de mujeres en la escuela primaria, 1990–95
Proporción entre el número de niñas en edad escolar oficial matriculadas en la escuela primaria y el número de niñas en edad escolar oficial.

Distribution of world population among economies grouped by female net primary enrollment ratio

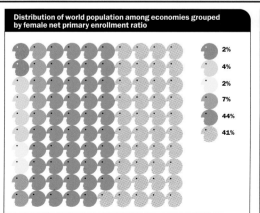

- 2%
- 4%
- 2%
- 7%
- 44%
- 41%

Females as percentage of total primary enrollment, 1994

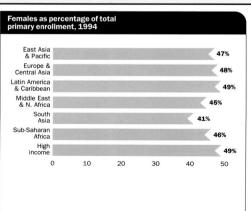

Region	%
East Asia & Pacific	47%
Europe & Central Asia	48%
Latin America & Caribbean	49%
Middle East & N. Africa	45%
South Asia	41%
Sub-Saharan Africa	46%
High income	49%

0   10   20   30   40   50

Female net primary enrollment ratio, 1990–95

	Economies	GNP $ millions 1996	Population millions 1996	GNP per capita $ 1996
Less than 40%	9	23,945	142	170
40%–59%	10	52,759	225	230
60%–79%	12	292,554	109	2,680
80%–94%	35	1,608,484	410	3,920
95% or more	49	23,216,120	2,499	9,290
No data	95	4,315,752	2,368	1,820

Private consumption per capita growth rate, 1990–96

The average annual percentage change in a country's private consumption per capita.

Taux de croissance de la consommation privée par habitant, 1990–96
Taux moyen annuel de variation de la consommation privée par habitant.

Tasa de crecimiento per cápita del consumo privado, 1990-96
Variación porcentual anual media del consumo privado per cápita de un país.

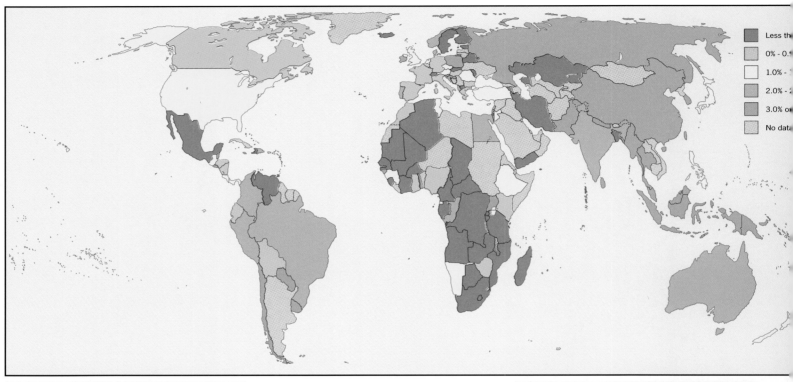

Legend:
- Less th[an]
- 0% - 0.[9]
- 1.0% - [1]
- 2.0% - [2]
- 3.0% o[r]
- No dat[a]

Distribution of world population among economies grouped by private consumption

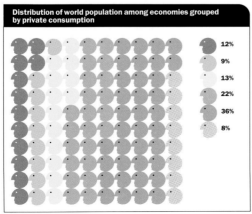

- 12%
- 9%
- 13%
- 22%
- 36%
- 8%

Private consumption per capita growth rate, 1990–96

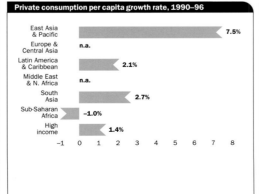

East Asia & Pacific	7.5%
Europe & Central Asia	n.a.
Latin America & Caribbean	2.1%
Middle East & N. Africa	n.a.
South Asia	2.7%
Sub-Saharan Africa	–1.0%
High income	1.4%

(scale: –1 0 1 2 3 4 5 6 7 8)

Annual growth of per capita private consumption, 1990–96, percent

	Economies	GNP $ millions 1996	Population millions 1996	GNP per capita $ 1996
Less than 0%	43	1,564,033	690	2,270
0%–0.9%	20	6,747,596	535	12,620
1.0%–1.9%	20	14,847,502	743	19,990
2.0%–2.9%	14	2,082,673	1,277	1,630
3.0% or more	32	3,309,314	2,058	1,610
No data	81	958,495	452	2,120

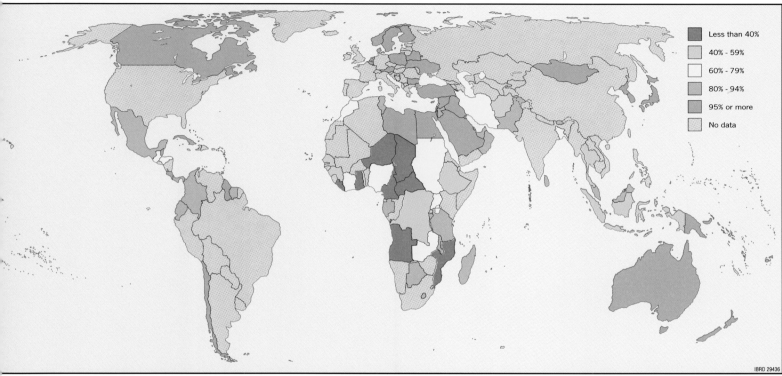

■	Less than 40%
░	40% - 59%
□	60% - 79%
▒	80% - 94%
▓	95% or more
░	No data

IBRD 29436

The share of the population that can expect to receive treatment for common diseases and injuries, including essential drugs on the national list, within one hour's walk or travel.

Accès aux soins de santé, 1993
Pourcentage de la population qui peut compter recevoir des soins pour des maladies ou blessures ordinaires, notamment grâce aux médicaments essentiels figurant sur la liste nationale, dans un endroit situé à une heure de trajet ou moins.

Acceso a la atención de salud, 1993
El porcentaje de la población que puede esperar recibir tratamiento médico por enfermedades y lesiones comunes, incluidos los medicamentos esenciales comprendidos en la lista nacional, en un centro al que pueda llegar en un máximo de una hora caminando o por otros medios.

Distribution of world population among economies grouped by access to health care

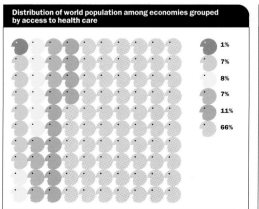

- 1%
- 7%
- 8%
- 7%
- 11%
- 66%

Access to health care in selected countries, percentage of population

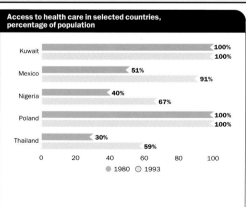

Kuwait	100% / 100%
Mexico	51% / 91%
Nigeria	40% / 67%
Poland	100% / 100%
Thailand	30% / 59%

0   20   40   60   80   100

● 1980   ○ 1993

Access to health care, 1993, percentage of population with access

	Economies	GNP $ millions 1996	Population millions 1996	GNP per capita $ 1996
Less than 40%	8	24,338	82	300
40%–59%	10	422,974	414	1,020
60%–79%	13	265,751	427	620
80%–94%	24	717,844	389	1,840
95% or more	51	9,601,518	655	14,670
No data	104	18,477,188	3,786	4,880

Economy	Population thousands 1996	Population growth rate % per year 1990–96	Private consumption per capita average annual growth % 1990–96	Health care % of population with access 1993	Life expectancy at birth years 1996	Infant mortality rate per 1,000 live births 1996	Child malnutrition % under-weight 1990–96[a]	Net female primary enrollment % 1990–95[b]	Female labor force % of total 1996
Afghanistan	24,167	2.8	..	40	45	156	40	8	35
Albania	3,286	0.0	8.4	..	72	37	..	97	41
Algeria	28,734	2.3	–1.5	..	70	32	10	91	25
American Samoa	60	4.0	..	..	..	..	..	..	..
Andorra	71	..	..	..	..	..	..	..	..
Angola	11,100	3.1	–6.7	24	46	124	35	..	46
Antigua and Barbuda	66	0.4	..	100	75	18	10	..	..
Argentina	35,220	1.3	..	..	73	22	2	..	31
Armenia	3,774	1.0	–18.6	..	73	16	..	..	48
Aruba	77	2.7	..	..	..	..	..	..	..
Australia	18,312	1.2	2.3	100	78	6	..	98	43
Austria	8,059	0.7	1.3	100	77	5	..	100	41
Azerbaijan	7,581	1.0	..	..	69	20	10	..	44
Bahamas, The	284	1.7	..	100	73	18	..	96	46
Bahrain	599	2.9	..	100	73	18	7	100	19
Bangladesh	121,671	1.6	–0.8	74	58	77	68	58	42
Barbados	264	0.4	..	100	76	11	6	78	46
Belarus	10,298	0.1	–7.9	100	69	13	..	94	49
Belgium	10,159	0.3	0.8	100	77	7	..	98	40
Belize	222	2.7	3.0	95	75	35	6	98	22
Benin	5,632	2.9	..	42	55	87	24	43	48
Bermuda	62	0.4	..	..	75	..	..	..	..
Bhutan	715	2.9	..	80	53	107	38	..	40
Bolivia	7,588	2.4	0.7	..	61	67	16	87	37
Bosnia and Herzegovina	..	..	..	..	..	..	..	..	38
Botswana	1,480	2.5	–5.7	86	51	56	27	99	46
Brazil	161,365	1.4	2.9	..	67	36	7	..	35
Brunei	290	2.0	..	..	75	10	..	91	34
Bulgaria	8,356	–0.7	0.8	100	71	16	..	96	48
Burkina Faso	10,669	2.8	–0.1	..	46	98	33	24	47
Burundi	6,423	2.6	–5.4	80	47	97	38	48	49
Cambodia	10,275	2.8	..	..	53	105	38	..	53
Cameroon	13,676	2.9	–5.6	15	56	54	15	..	38
Canada	29,964	1.3	0.3	99	79	6	..	94	45
Cape Verde	389	2.2	2.2	82	66	43	19	100	38
Cayman Islands	32	..	..	..	..	..	..	..	..
Central African Republic	3,344	2.2	–2.1	13	49	96	23	43	47
Chad	6,611	2.5	–2.3	26	48	115	..	..	44
Channel Islands	148	0.7	..	..	78	7	..	..	..
Chile	14,419	1.6	7.1	95	75	12	1	85	32
China	1,215,414	1.1	9.6	..	70	33	16	98	45
Hong Kong, China	6,311	1.7	4.2	..	79	4	..	92	37
Colombia	37,451	1.8	2.7	87	70	25	8	..	38
Comoros	505	2.6	0.3	..	59	67	..	48	42
Congo, Dem. Rep.	45,234	3.2	–9.9	59	53	90	34	50	44
Congo, Rep.	2,705	2.9	2.5	..	51	90	24	..	43
Costa Rica	3,442	2.1	1.4	97	77	12	2	87	30
Côte d'Ivoire	14,347	3.0	–2.6	60	54	84	24	..	33
Croatia	4,771	0.0	3.5	..	72	9	..	82	44
Cuba	11,019	0.6	..	100	76	8	8	99	38
Cyprus	740	1.4	1.1	100	77	8	..	96	38
Czech Republic	10,315	–0.1	1.2	..	74	6	1	98	47
Denmark	5,262	0.4	2.6	100	75	6	..	99	46
Djibouti	619	3.0	..	..	50	108	23	28	..
Dominica	74	0.3	..	100	74	16	..	..	..
Dominican Republic	7,964	1.9	2.5	..	71	40	6	83	29
Ecuador	11,698	2.2	0.5	80	70	34	17	92	27
Egypt, Arab Rep.	59,272	2.0	2.1	99	65	53	9	82	29
El Salvador	5,810	2.4	4.7	..	69	34	11	80	35
Equatorial Guinea	410	2.6	1.1	..	50	109	..	..	35
Eritrea	3,698	2.7	..	..	55	64	41	30	47
Estonia	1,466	–1.2	–2.3	..	69	10	..	94	49
Ethiopia	58,234	2.2	1.6	55	49	109	48	19	41
Faeroe Islands	47	..	..	..	..	..	..	..	..
Fiji	803	1.5	..	99	72	18	8	100	28
Finland	5,125	0.5	–0.9	100	77	4	..	99	48
France	58,375	0.5	0.8	..	78	5	..	99	44
French Guiana	153	..	..	..	..	..	..	..	..
French Polynesia	220	1.9	..	..	72	16	..	100	..
Gabon	1,125	2.6	–4.9	87	55	87	15	..	44
Gambia, The	1,147	3.7	3.4	..	53	79	17	46	45
Georgia	5,411	–0.2	..	..	72	17	..	82	46
Germany	81,912	0.5	0.9	..	76	5	..	100	42
Ghana	17,522	2.7	0.7	25	59	71	27	..	51
Greece	10,475	0.5	0.8	..	78	8	..	98	37
Greenland	58	0.6	..	..	68	24	..	..	..
Grenada	99	1.4	2.8	..	..	14	..	..	..
Guadeloupe	422	1.3	..	..	75	8	..	..	45
Guam	153	2.3	..	..	74	12	..	..	..
Guatemala	10,928	2.9	1.5	60	66	41	33	..	27
Guinea	6,759	2.7	1.7	45	46	122	24	..	47
Guinea-Bissau	1,094	2.1	4.9	..	44	134	23	..	40
Guyana	839	0.9	..	96	64	59	18	89	33
Haiti	7,336	2.1	–2.6	45	55	72	28	26	43
Honduras	6,101	3.0	0.3	62	67	44	18	91	30
Hungary	10,193	–0.3	0.5	..	70	11	..	94	44
Iceland	270	1.0	–1.6	..	79	6	..	..	44
India	945,121	1.8	2.8	..	63	65	66	..	32
Indonesia	197,055	1.7	5.5	43	65	49	40	95	40
Iran, Islamic Rep.	62,509	2.5	–0.4	73	70	36	16	..	25
Iraq	21,366	2.8	..	98	62	101	12	74	18
Ireland	3,626	0.6	3.4	..	76	5	..	100	33
Isle of Man	72	..	..	..	..	..	..	..	..
Israel	5,692	3.3	4.2	100	77	6	..	..	40
Italy	57,380	0.2	0.1	..	78	6	..	..	38
Jamaica	2,547	1.0	4.6	..	74	12	10	100	46
Japan	125,761	0.3	1.7	100	80	4	3	100	41
Jordan	4,312	5.1	1.2	90	71	30	10	89	22
Kazakhstan	16,471	–0.3	–4.5	..	65	25	1	..	47
Kenya	27,364	2.6	0.4	..	58	57	23	..	46
Kiribati	82	2.0	..	100	60	64	..	..	..
Korea, Dem. Rep.	22,451	1.6	..	100	63	56	..	..	45
Korea, Rep.	45,545	1.0	6.1	100	72	9	..	99	41
Kuwait	1,590	–4.8	..	100	77	11	6	65	29
Kyrgyz Republic	4,576	0.7	..	..	67	26	..	95	47
Lao PDR	4,726	2.6	..	..	53	101	40	61	47
Latvia	2,490	–1.2	..	..	69	16	..	82	50
Lebanon	4,079	1.9	6.6	..	70	31	9	..	28
Lesotho	2,023	2.1	–5.0	80	58	74	21	71	37
Liberia	2,810	2.4	..	34	49	162	20	..	39
Libya	5,167	2.5	..	100	68	25	5	96	21
Liechtenstein	31	..	..	..	..	..	..	..	..

Economy	Population thousands 1996	Population growth rate % per year 1990–96	Private consumption per capita average annual growth % 1990–96	Health care % of population with access 1993	Life expectancy at birth years 1996	Infant mortality rate per 1,000 live births 1996	Child malnutrition % under-weight 1990–96[a]	Net female primary enrollment % 1990–95[b]	Female labor force % of total 1996
Lithuania	3,709	–0.1	..	..	70	10	..	..	48
Luxembourg	416	1.4	0.6	100	77	5	..	..	37
Macao	461	3.6	2.9	..	77	5	..	82	39
Macedonia, FYR	1,980	0.7	–6.0	..	72	16	..	84	41
Madagascar	13,705	2.7	–2.0	65	58	88	32	..	45
Malawi	10,016	2.7	–1.0	80	43	133	28	100	49
Malaysia	20,565	2.3	4.8	88	72	11	23	92	37
Maldives	256	2.9	..	75	64	49	39	..	42
Mali	9,999	2.8	–1.7	..	50	120	31	19	46
Malta	373	0.9	..	..	77	11	..	99	27
Marshall Islands	57	3.5	..	..	..	26	..	..	..
Martinique	384	1.1	..	..	77	7	..	..	47
Mauritania	2,332	2.5	–1.4	..	53	94	48	55	44
Mauritius	1,134	1.2	3.7	99	71	17	15	96	32
Mayotte	108	..	..	..	..	..	..	..	..
Mexico	93,182	1.8	–1.5	91	72	32	14	..	31
Micronesia, Fed. Sts.	109	2.1	..	75	66	31	..	..	38
Moldova	4,327	–0.1	–14.8	..	67	20	..	..	49
Monaco	32	..	..	..	..	..	..	..	..
Mongolia	2,516	2.1	..	100	65	53	12	81	46
Morocco	27,020	1.9	0.8	62	66	53	10	62	35
Mozambique	18,028	4.0	–2.6	30	45	123	47	35	48
Myanmar	45,883	1.7	3.4	..	60	80	31	..	43
Namibia	1,584	2.6	1.5	..	56	61	26	..	41
Nepal	22,037	2.7	6.1	..	57	85	49	..	40
Netherlands	15,517	0.6	1.4	100	77	5	..	99	40
Netherlands Antilles	202	1.1	..	..	76	11	..	..	42
New Caledonia	197	2.7	..	..	74	11	..	99	..
New Zealand	3,635	1.3	1.6	100	76	6	..	100	44
Nicaragua	4,503	3.1	0.1	..	68	44	24	85	36
Niger	9,335	3.3	..	30	47	118	43	18	44
Nigeria	114,568	2.9	0.2	67	53	78	35	..	36
Northern Mariana Islands	63	..	..	..	..	..	..	..	..
Norway	4,381	0.5	2.0	100	78	4	..	99	46
Oman	2,173	4.8	..	89	71	18	14	70	15
Pakistan	133,510	2.9	3.1	85	63	88	40	..	27
Palau	17	..	..	..	..	..	..	..	..
Panama	2,674	1.8	1.0	82	74	22	7	92	34
Papua New Guinea	4,401	2.3	4.7	96	58	62	30	..	42
Paraguay	4,955	2.7	3.3	..	71	24	4	89	29
Peru	24,288	2.0	2.7	..	68	42	11	90	29
Philippines	71,899	2.3	1.8	..	66	37	30	..	37
Poland	38,618	0.2	4.6	100	72	12	..	96	46
Portugal	9,930	0.1	2.1	..	75	7	..	100	43
Puerto Rico	3,783	1.2	..	..	75	12	..	..	36
Qatar	658	5.0	..	100	72	18	6	80	13
Reunion	664	1.7	..	..	75	7	..	..	42
Romania	22,608	–0.4	1.4	..	69	22	6	92	44
Russian Federation	147,739	–0.1	5.9	..	66	17	3	100	49
Rwanda	6,727	–0.6	–4.6	..	41	129	29	76	49
Samoa	172	1.2	..	100	69	23	..	99	..
São Tomé and Principe	135	2.7	–3.8	88	64	50	17	..	..
Saudi Arabia	19,409	3.4	..	98	70	22	..	61	14
Senegal	8,534	2.5	–1.3	40	50	60	22	48	43
Seychelles	77	1.5	13.5	99	71	18	6	..	..
Sierra Leone	4,630	2.4	–1.3	..	37	174	29	..	36
Singapore	3,044	2.0	5.1	100	76	4	14	..	38
Slovak Republic	5,343	0.2	–3.9	..	73	11	..	..	48
Slovenia	1,991	–0.1	5.5	..	74	5	..	99	46
Solomon Islands	389	3.3	..	80	63	39	21	..	46
Somalia	9,805	2.1	..	..	49	127	39	..	43
South Africa	37,643	1.7	–0.1	..	65	49	9	96	37
Spain	39,260	0.2	0.7	..	77	5	..	100	36
Sri Lanka	18,300	1.2	4.7	90	73	15	38	..	35
St. Kitts and Nevis	41	–0.5	..	100	70	24	..	..	..
St. Lucia	158	1.0	..	100	70	17	..	..	..
St. Vincent & the Grenadines	112	0.7	..	80	73	18	..	..	..
Sudan	27,272	2.1	..	70	54	74	34	..	29
Suriname	432	1.1	..	91	71	25	..	..	32
Swaziland	926	3.1	..	55	57	67	10	96	37
Sweden	8,843	0.5	–0.7	100	79	4	..	100	48
Switzerland	7,074	0.9	–0.4	100	78	5	..	100	40
Syrian Arab Republic	14,502	3.0	..	99	69	31	..	87	26
Tajikistan	5,927	1.9	..	..	69	32	..	..	44
Tanzania	30,494	3.0	–0.8	93	50	86	29	48	49
Thailand	60,003	1.3	6.6	59	69	34	13	..	46
Togo	4,230	3.0	–1.9	..	50	87	25	72	40
Tonga	97	0.2	..	100	72	14	..	..	..
Trinidad and Tobago	1,297	0.8	–1.1	99	73	13	7	94	37
Tunisia	9,132	1.9	1.8	90	70	30	9	95	31
Turkey	62,697	1.8	1.5	100	69	42	10	94	36
Turkmenistan	4,598	3.8	..	..	66	41	..	..	45
Uganda	19,741	3.2	3.6	71	43	99	26	..	48
Ukraine	50,718	–0.4	..	100	67	14	..	..	49
United Arab Emirates	2,532	5.3	..	90	75	15	7	82	14
United Kingdom	58,782	0.3	1.1	..	77	6	..	100	43
United States	265,284	1.0	1.5	..	77	7	..	97	46
Uruguay	3,203	0.6	9.4	..	74	18	4	95	41
Uzbekistan	23,228	2.1	..	..	69	24	..	..	46
Vanuatu	173	2.7	..	80	64	39	..	..	..
Venezuela	22,311	2.2	–0.8	..	73	22	5	90	33
Vietnam	75,355	2.2	..	..	68	40	45	..	49
Virgin Islands (U.S.)	98	–0.6	..	..	76	13	..	..	..
West Bank and Gaza	2,279	5.5	..	..	68	..	38	..	..
Yemen, Rep.	15,778	4.7	–3.8	..	54	98	30	..	29
Yugoslavia, FR (Serb./Mont.)	10,574	0.1	..	..	72	14	..	70	42
Zambia	9,215	2.8	–7.1	75	44	112	29	76	45
Zimbabwe	11,248	2.4	0.1	..	56	56	16	..	44

.. Not available.

Note: Figures in italics are for years other than those specified; 0 or 0.0 means zero or less than half the unit shown and not known more precisely.

a. Data refer to any year from 1990 to 1996. b. Data refer to any year from 1990 to 1995.

Environment

Where developing countries are making economic progress, they risk repeating the mistakes of the past by putting growth before the environment—because growth can be a two-edged sword. Although economic growth raises living standards and gives people the means to enjoy their environment, it is often accompanied by urbanization, more motor vehicles, and increased energy consumption. And because unbridled growth can lead to congestion, overloaded infrastructure, and dangerous declines in air and water quality, growth at the expense of the environment is likely to be unsustainable.

The pace of change is putting increasing pressure on the world's environmental resources. Much of the world's biological diversity is in developing nations, and it is estimated to be disappearing at 50 to 100 times natural rates. Wetlands and forests are being lost at 0.3 to 1.0 percent a year. Greenhouse gas emissions are growing strongly with increasing economic activity. Reversing these trends will require actions by both industrial and developing countries.

Many governments are adopting policies for sustainable development—that is, development that preserves the opportunities for well-being of both current and future generations. Economic growth and better environmental management can be complementary, because growth provides the resources to improve the environment. Striking a better balance between the costs and benefits of economic development requires reliable information to guide policies and track progress toward sustainable development.

Understanding the environment and its links to economic activities requires a sound base of data and indicators. Some indicators deal with environmental "goods" such as protected areas or biodiversity. Others measure "bads" such as deforestation, soil loss, or air and water pollution. Still others monitor the effects of environmental degradation—waterborne disease, species loss, and numbers of threatened species. Such indicators help document the links between the environment and the economy.

Environnement

Les pays en développement qui progressent sur le plan économique risquent de répéter les erreurs du passé en faisant passer la croissance avant l'environnement, car la croissance peut-être une arme à double tranchant. Si elle a pour effet d'améliorer les niveaux de vie et de donner aux gens les moyens de profiter de leur environnement, la croissance économique est souvent synonyme d'urbanisation, d'augmentation du nombre des véhicules à moteur et d'accroissement de la consommation d'énergie. Et comme elle peut, si elle est incontrôlée, être cause de congestion, d'une surcharge des infrastructures et d'une baisse dangereuse de la qualité de l'air et de l'eau, la croissance qui se fait au détriment de l'environnement risque de ne pas être viable.

Le rythme du changement exerce une pression croissante sur les ressources environnementales de notre planète. La diversité biologique est localisée pour une bonne part dans les pays en développement, et l'on estime qu'elle disparaît aujourd'hui à un rythme de 50 à 100 fois supérieur aux taux naturels. Le recul des zones humides et des forêts est de l'ordre de 0,3 à 1,0 % par an. Les émissions de gaz à effet de serre augmentent fortement du fait de l'accélération de l'activité économique. Pour inverser ces tendances, il faudra que des mesures soient prises à la fois par les pays industrialisés et par les pays en développement.

Nombreux sont les États qui adoptent aujourd'hui des politiques visant à assurer un développement durable, c'est-à-dire un développement qui préserve les chances de bien-être des générations actuelles et futures. La croissance économique et l'amélioration de la gestion environnementale peuvent être complémentaires, car la croissance fournit les ressources dont on a besoin pour améliorer l'environnement. Assurer un meilleur équilibre entre les coûts et les avantages du développement économique suppose que l'on dispose d'informations fiables pour orienter les politiques et suivre les progrès réalisés dans le sens d'un développement durable.

Pour comprendre l'environnement et ses interactions avec l'activités économique, il faut disposer d'une bonne base de données et d'indicateurs. Certains indicateurs ont trait aux « bienfaits » environnementaux, comme la biodiversité ou les aires protégées. D'autres mesurent des « méfaits » tels que le déboisement, l'érosion des sols ou la pollution de l'air et de l'eau. D'autres encore permettent de contrôler les effets des dégradations de l'environnement — maladies hydriques, disparitions d'espèces ou nombre d'espèces menacées. Tous ces indicateurs permettent de documenter les liens qui existent entre l'environnement et l'économie.

Medio Ambiente

En los casos en que los países en desarrollo están logrando progresos económicos, se corre el riesgo de repetir los errores del pasado si los objetivos de crecimiento priman sobre el medio ambiente, ya que el crecimiento económico puede ser una espada de dos filos. Al tiempo que mejora la calidad de vida y brinda a la población los medios para que disfrute del medio ambiente, el crecimiento económico suele ir acompañado de un proceso de urbanización, un aumento del parque de automóviles y un mayor consumo de energía. Un crecimiento desbocado puede dar lugar a congestión, sobrecarga de la infraestructura y una disminución peligrosa de la calidad del aire y del agua, por lo que un crecimiento que se produzca a expensas del medio ambiente será, probablemente, insostenible.

El ritmo con que se producen los cambios está ejerciendo cada vez más presión sobre los recursos ambientales del planeta. Gran parte de la diversidad biológica se encuentra en países en desarrollo, y se estima que la tasa de desaparición es entre 50 y 100 veces más rápida de lo que sería natural. Las marismas y los bosques se están perdiendo a un ritmo anual de 0,3% a 1,0%. Las emisiones de gases que producen el efecto invernadero están aumentado significativamente al incrementarse la actividad económica. Para invertir estas tendencias será menester que tanto los países desarrollados como los países en desarrollo tomen las medidas oportunas.

Muchos gobiernos están adoptando políticas enfocadas al desarrollo sostenible, es decir, un desarrollo que preserve las oportunidades de bienestar tanto de nuestra generación como de las generaciones futuras. El crecimiento económico y una mejor gestión del medio ambiente pueden ser factores complementarios, porque el crecimiento proporciona los recursos para mejorar el medio ambiente. Para lograr un mayor equilibrio entre los costos y los beneficios del desarrollo económico se necesita información fiable, a fin de orientar las políticas y registrar los avances conseguidos hacia el desarrollo sostenible.

Para entender el medio ambiente y sus relaciones con las actividades económicas se requiere una sólida base de datos e indicadores. Algunos indicadores se refieren a los "bienes" ambientales, como las zonas protegidas o la biodiversidad. Otros miden los "males", como la deforestación, la desaparición del suelo o la contaminación del aire y del agua. Un tercer grupo permite supervisar los efectos de la degradación ambiental: enfermedades transmitidas por el agua, desaparición de especies y número de especies amenazadas. Estos indicadores ayudan a documentar las relaciones entre medio ambiente y economía.

Forest coverage, 1995

The percentage of total land area that is covered by forest.

Couvert forestier, 1995

Superficie boisée en pourcentage de la superficie totale des terres.

Cubierta forestal, 1995

Porcentaje de la superficie continental del planeta que está cubierta de bosques.

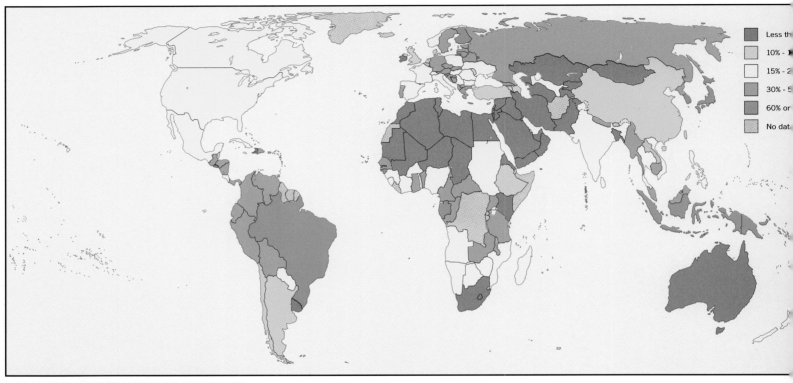

■	Less th
▨	10% -
□	15% - 2
▨	30% - 5
■	60% or
▨	No dat

Distribution of world population among economies grouped by forest coverage

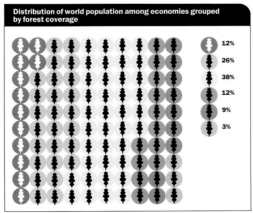

	12%
	26%
	38%
	12%
	9%
	3%

Forest coverage, 1995, percentage of land area

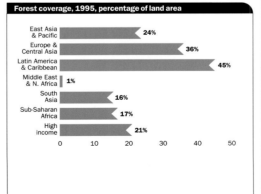

- East Asia & Pacific — 24%
- Europe & Central Asia — 36%
- Latin America & Caribbean — 45%
- Middle East & N. Africa — 1%
- South Asia — 16%
- Sub-Saharan Africa — 17%
- High income — 21%

(scale: 0 10 20 30 40 50)

Forest coverage, 1995, percentage of land area

	Economies	GNP $ millions 1996	Population millions 1996	GNP per capita $ 1996
Less than 10%	39	1,564,437	715	2,190
10%–14%	13	3,189,366	1,494	2,130
15%–29%	38	13,187,633	2,155	6,120
30%–59%	45	4,032,222	705	5,720
60% or more	8	6,684,139	541	12,340
No data	67	851,817	143	5,980

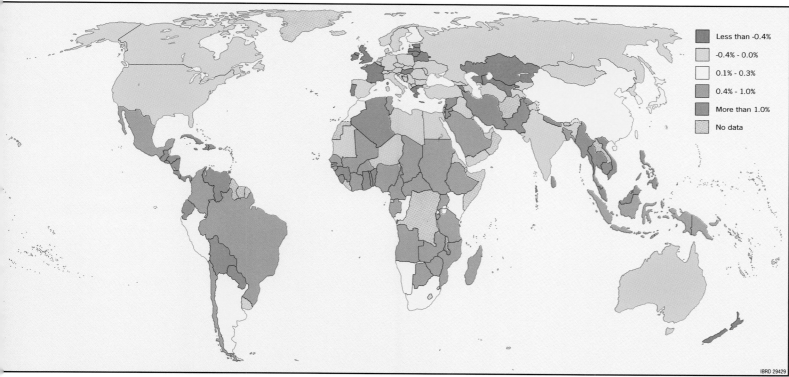

Less than -0.4%

-0.4% - 0.0%

0.1% - 0.3%

0.4% - 1.0%

More than 1.0%

No data

IBRD 29429

The average annual percentage change in forest area. Negative numbers indicate an increase in forest area.

Déboisement annuel, 1990–95
Variation annuelle moyenne de la superficie boisée, en pourcentage. Un chiffre négatif indique une augmentation de la superficie boisée.

Deforestación anual, 1990–95
Variación porcentual anual media en la superficie cubierta de bosques. Las cifras con signo negativo indican un aumento de dicha superficie.

Distribution of world population among economies grouped by annual deforestation

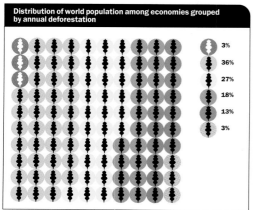

3%

36%

27%

18%

13%

3%

Annual deforestation, 1990–95, thousands of square kilometers

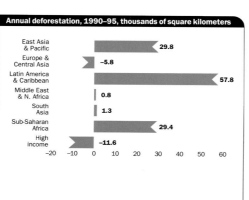

East Asia & Pacific	29.8
Europe & Central Asia	−5.8
Latin America & Caribbean	57.8
Middle East & N. Africa	0.8
South Asia	1.3
Sub-Saharan Africa	29.4
High income	−11.6

-20 -10 0 10 20 30 40 50 60

Annual deforestation, 1990–95, percent per year

	Economies	GNP $ millions 1996	Population millions 1996	GNP per capita $ 1996
Less than −0.4%	14	3,159,396	216	14,600
−0.4% to 0.0%	49	15,666,997	2,053	7,630
0.1% to 0.3%	12	7,193,984	1,554	4,630
0.4% to 1.0%	32	1,747,001	1,054	1,660
More than 1.0%	35	879,423	731	1,200
No data	68	862,812	145	5,960

Energy efficiency, 1995

Gross domestic product divided by total energy consumption in oil equivalents, expressed in constant 1987 U.S. dollars.

Rendement énergétique, 1995
Produit intérieur brut divisé par la consommation totale d'énergie en équivalent pétrole, exprimé en dollars constants des États-Unis aux prix de 1987.

Eficiencia del uso de la energía, 1995
Producto interno bruto dividido por el consumo total de energía en el equivalente en petróleo, expresado en dólares constantes de EE.UU. de 1987.

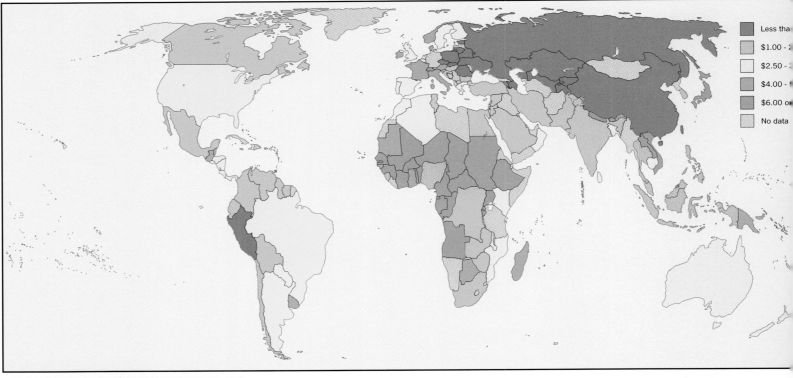

Less tha
$1.00 -
$2.50 -
$4.00 -
$6.00 o
No data

Distribution of world population among economies grouped by GDP per kilogram of energy used

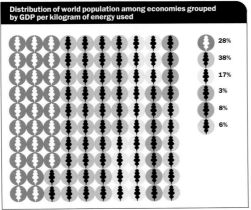

28%	
38%	
17%	
3%	
8%	
6%	

GDP per kilogram of energy used, 1995 (1987 $)

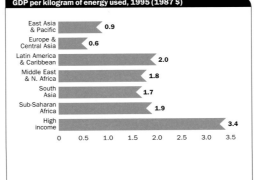

East Asia & Pacific	0.9
Europe & Central Asia	0.6
Latin America & Caribbean	2.0
Middle East & N. Africa	1.8
South Asia	1.7
Sub-Saharan Africa	1.9
High income	3.4

GDP per kilogram of energy used, 1995 (1987 $)

	Economies	GNP $ millions 1996	Population millions 1996	GNP per capita $ 1996
Less than $1.00	19	1,710,982	1,594	1,070
$1.00–$2.49	41	3,564,781	2,190	1,630
$2.50–$3.99	43	12,429,153	972	12,790
$4.00–$5.99	22	3,526,370	204	17,270
$6.00 or more	34	5,576,117	465	11,990
No data	51	2,702,211	328	8,230

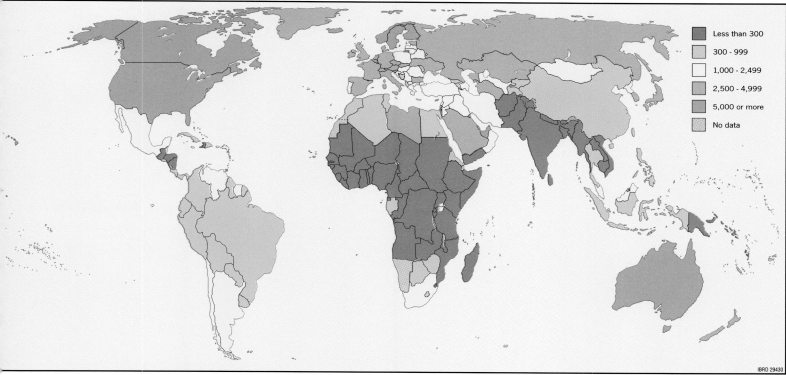

■	Less than 300	
■	300 - 999	
□	1,000 - 2,499	
■	2,500 - 4,999	
■	5,000 or more	
▒	No data	

IBRD 29430

Annual consumption of commercial energy divided by population, expressed in kilograms of oil equivalent.

Consommation d'énergie par habitant, 1995
Consommation annuelle d'énergie commerciale du pays divisée par le nombre d'habitants, exprimée en kilogrammes d'équivalent pétrole.

Consumo de energía per cápita, 1995
Consumo anual de energía comercial dividido por la población, expresado en kilogramos de equivalente en petróleo.

Distribution of world population among economies grouped by energy use per capita

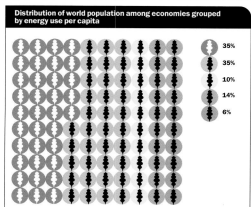

- 35%
- 35%
- 10%
- 14%
- 6%

Energy use per capita, 1995, kilograms of oil equivalent

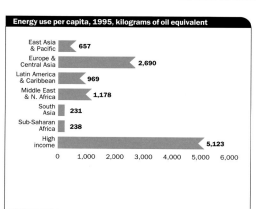

East Asia & Pacific	657
Europe & Central Asia	2,690
Latin America & Caribbean	969
Middle East & N. Africa	1,178
South Asia	231
Sub-Saharan Africa	238
High income	5,123

0 1,000 2,000 3,000 4,000 5,000 6,000

Energy use per capita, 1995, kilograms of oil equivalent

	Economies	GNP $ millions 1996	Population millions 1996	GNP per capita $ 1996
Less than 300	61	688,946	1,987	350
300–999	45	2,566,063	2,002	1,280
1,000–2,499	37	2,142,956	590	3,630
2,500–4,999	30	14,725,191	810	18,180
5,000 or more	20	9,363,667	354	26,490
No data	17	22,791	11	2,150

Annual water use per capita, 1980–96

A country's annual water use, in a single year, divided by its population of the same year and expressed in cubic meters.

Consommation d'eau annuelle par habitant, 1980–96

Consommation d'eau annuelle d'un pays, calculée pour une année donnée, divisée par la population de ce pays au cours de l'année en question et exprimée en mètres cubes.

Consumo anual de agua per cápita, 1980–96

Consumo anual de agua de un país en un solo año, dividido por su número de habitantes en el mismo año y expresado en metros cúbicos.

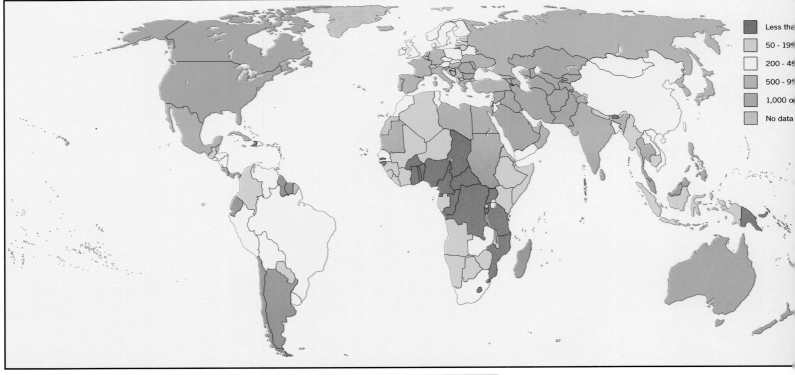

Less tha

50 - 19

200 - 4

500 - 9

1,000 o

No data

Distribution of world population among economies grouped by annual water use per capita

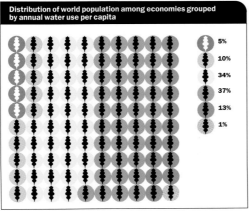

5%

10%

34%

37%

13%

1%

Freshwater resources available per capita, 1996, thousands of cubic meters

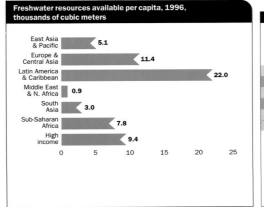

East Asia & Pacific	5.1
Europe & Central Asia	11.4
Latin America & Caribbean	22.0
Middle East & N. Africa	0.9
South Asia	3.0
Sub-Saharan Africa	7.8
High income	9.4

0   5   10   15   20   25

Annual water use per capita, 1980–96, cubic meters

	Economies	GNP $ millions 1996	Population millions 1996	GNP per capita $ 1996
Less than 50	22	82,795	317	260
50–199	33	883,262	569	1,550
200–499	36	4,514,121	1,946	2,320
500–999	37	14,507,499	2,120	6,840
1,000 or more	22	8,877,965	730	12,170
No data	60	643,972	72	8,920

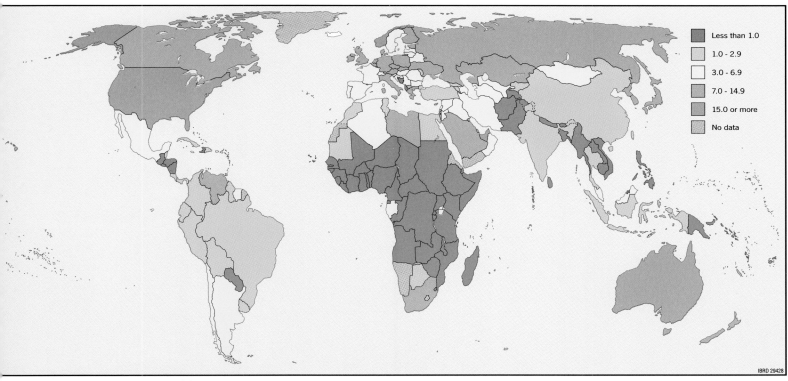

■	Less than 1.0
■	1.0 - 2.9
□	3.0 - 6.9
■	7.0 - 14.9
■	15.0 or more
■	No data

IBRD 29428

Emissions of CO_2 from the burning of fossil fuels and the manufacture of cement, divided by population, expressed in metric tons.

Émissions de dioxyde de carbone par habitant, 1995
Émissions de CO_2 produites par les combustibles utilisés dans les procédés industriels et la fabrication de ciment, divisées par la population, exprimées en tonnes.

Emisiones de dióxido de carbono per cápita, 1995
Emisiones de CO_2 producidas por los combustibles fósiles y la fabricación de cemento, dividi-das por la población, expre-sadas en toneladas métricas.

Distribution of world population among economies grouped by carbon dioxide emssions per capita

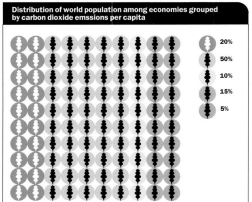

- 20%
- 50%
- 10%
- 15%
- 5%

Carbon dioxide emissions per capita, 1995, metric tons

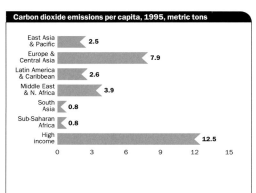

East Asia & Pacific	2.5
Europe & Central Asia	7.9
Latin America & Caribbean	2.6
Middle East & N. Africa	3.9
South Asia	0.8
Sub-Saharan Africa	0.8
High income	12.5

0   3   6   9   12   15

Carbon dioxide emissions per capita, 1995, metric tons

	Economies	GNP $ millions 1996	Population millions 1996	GNP per capita $ 1996
Less than 1.0	66	444,893	1,133	390
1.0–2.9	29	2,924,645	2,872	1,020
3.0–6.9	39	4,229,071	553	7,640
7.0–14.9	30	13,420,816	847	15,850
15.0 or more	10	8,157,053	297	27,460
No data	36	333,136	52	6,460

Economy	Land area thousand sq. km 1995	Annual water use % of total water resources[b] 1980–96	Annual water use Per capita cubic m 1980–96	Forest coverage Total area thousand sq. km 1995	Forest coverage As % of total land area 1995	Forest coverage Average annual deforestation % 1990–95	Energy use Per capita kg 1995	Energy use GDP per kilogram oil equivalent constant 1987 $ 1995	Carbon dioxide emissions per capita metric tons 1995
Afghanistan	652.1	47.1	1,825	..	..	..	111	..	0.1
Albania	27.4	0.4[c]	94	10	38	0.0	314	1.8	0.6
Algeria	2,381.7	32.4	180	19	1	1.2	866	2.7	3.2
American Samoa	0.2	..	..	..	..	..	906	..	..
Andorra	0.5	..	..	..	..	..	..	..	..
Angola	1,246.7	0.3	57	222	18	1.0	89	7.7	0.4
Antigua and Barbuda	0.4	..	..	..	..	..	2,025	2.9	..
Argentina	2,736.7	4.0[c]	1,043	339	12	0.3	1,525	2.5	3.7
Armenia	28.2	41.8	804	3	12	-2.7	444	0.6	1.0
Aruba	0.2	..	..	..	..	..	..	..	..
Australia	7,682.3	4.3[c]	933	409	5	0.0	5,215	2.8	16.0
Austria	82.7	4.2	304	39	47	0.0	3,279	5.5	7.4
Azerbaijan	86.6	195.1	2,177	10	11	0.0	1,735	0.2	5.7
Bahamas, The	10.0	..	..	..	..	..	6,781	1.5	6.1
Bahrain	0.7	..	..	..	..	..	9,716	0.8	25.7
Bangladesh	130.2	1.7	217	10	8	0.8	67	3.0	0.2
Barbados	0.4	..	..	..	..	..	1,007	5.7	3.1
Belarus	207.5	8.1	264	74	36	-1.0	2,305	0.7	5.7
Belgium	33.0[d]	107.5	917	..	..	..	5,167	3.2	10.2
Belize	22.8	0.1	109	..	..	..	411	5.2	1.9
Benin	110.6	1.5	28	46	42	1.2	20	18.4	0.1
Bermuda	0.1	..	..	..	..	..	2,885	7.3	..
Bhutan	47.0	0.0	13	..	..	..	33	17.3	0.3
Bolivia	1,084.4	0.4	201	483	45	1.2	396	2.0	1.4
Bosnia and Herzegovina	51.0	..	..	27	53	0.0	364	..	0.4
Botswana	566.7	3.8	84	139	25	0.5	383	5.1	1.5
Brazil	8,456.5	0.7	246	5,511	65	0.5	772	2.7	1.6
Brunei	5.3	..	..	..	..	..	11,368	1.0	28.9
Bulgaria	110.6	77.2	1,574	32	29	0.0	2,724	1.0	6.7
Burkina Faso	273.6	2.2	39	43	16	0.7	16	16.4	0.1
Burundi	25.7	2.8	20	3	12	0.4	23	7.7	0.0
Cambodia	176.5	0.6	66	98	56	1.6	52	2.6	0.0
Cameroon	465.4	0.1	38	196	42	0.6	117	6.1	0.3
Canada	9,221.0	1.6	1,602	2,446	27	-0.1	7,879	2.0	14.7
Cape Verde	4.0	..	..	..	..	..	303	3.0	0.3
Cayman Islands	0.3	..	..	..	..	..	..	..	..
Central African Republic	623.0	0.0	26	299	48	0.4	29	13.6	0.1
Chad	1,259.2	1.2	34	110	9	0.8	16	10.7	0.0
Channel Islands	..	..	..	..	..	..	..	..	..
Chile	748.8	3.6[c]	1,625	79	11	0.4	1,065	2.4	3.1
China	9,326.4	16.4	461	1,333	14	0.1	707	0.7	2.7
Hong Kong, China	1.0	..	..	..	..	..	2,212	5.4	5.0
Colombia	1,038.7	0.5	174	530	51	0.5	655	2.1	1.8
Comoros	2.2	..	..	..	..	..	39	10.9	0.1
Congo, Dem. Rep.	2,267.1	0.0	10	..	..	..	47	2.3	0.0
Congo, Rep.	341.5	0.0[c]	20	195	57	0.2	139	6.6	0.5
Costa Rica	51.1	1.4	780	12	24	3.0	584	3.3	1.6
Côte d'Ivoire	318.0	0.9	67	55	17	0.6	97	8.4	0.7
Croatia	55.9	..[c]	..	18	33	0.0	1,435	..	3.6
Cuba	109.8	23.5	870	18	17	1.2	949	..	2.6
Cyprus	9.2	..	..	..	..	..	2,663	2.8	7.1
Czech Republic	77.3	4.7	266	26	34	0.0	3,776	0.8	10.8
Denmark	42.4	10.9	233	4	10	0.0	3,918	5.7	10.5
Djibouti	23.2	..	..	..	..	..	922	..	0.6
Dominica	0.8	..	..	..	..	..	301	..	..
Dominican Republic	48.4	14.9	446	16	33	1.6	486	1.9	1.5

Economy	Land area thousand sq. km 1995	Annual water use % of total water resources[b] 1980–96	Annual water use Per capita cubic m 1980–96	Forest coverage Total area thousand sq. km 1995	Forest coverage As % of total land area 1995	Forest coverage Average annual deforestation % 1990–95	Energy use Per capita kg 1995	Energy use GDP per kilogram oil equivalent constant 1987 $ 1995	Carbon dioxide emissions per capita metric tons 1995
Ecuador	276.8	1.8	581	111	40	1.6	553	2.2	2.0
Egypt, Arab Rep.	995.5	1,967.9[c]	921	0	0	0.0	596	1.6	1.6
El Salvador	20.7	5.3	244	1	5	3.3	410	2.5	0.9
Equatorial Guinea	28.1	0.0	15	..	..	..	80	8.4	0.3
Eritrea	101.0	..	..	3	3	0.0	..	..	..
Estonia	42.3	26.0	107	20	48	-1.0	3,454	0.8	11.1
Ethiopia	1,000.0	2.0	51	136	14	0.5	21	7.4	0.1
Faeroe Islands	1.4	..	..	..	..	..	..	..	..
Fiji	18.3	0.1	42	..	..	..	515	3.8	0.9
Finland	304.6	2.0	440	200	66	0.1	5,613	3.3	10.0
France	550.1	21.0	665	150	27	-1.1	4,150	4.3	5.8
French Guiana	88.2	..	..	..	..	..	..	..	..
French Polynesia	3.7	..	..	..	..	..	1,428	..	..
Gabon	257.7	0.0	70	179	69	0.5	587	7.9	3.2
Gambia, The	10.0	0.7	29	1	9	0.9	55	4.4	0.2
Georgia	69.7	6.9	637	30	43	0.0	342	..	1.4
Germany	349.3	48.2[c]	580	107	31	0.0	4,156	..	10.2
Ghana	227.5	1.0	35	90	40	1.3	92	4.6	0.2
Greece	128.9	11.2	523	65	51	-2.3	2,266	2.8	7.3
Greenland	341.7	..	..	..	..	..	3,663	..	..
Grenada	0.3	..	..	..	..	..	284	7.1	..
Guadeloupe	1.7	..	..	..	..	..	634	..	..
Guam	0.6	..[c]	..	..	..	..	9,302	..	..
Guatemala	108.4	0.6	139	38	35	2.0	206	4.4	0.7
Guinea	245.7	0.3	142	64	26	1.1	64	6.7	0.2
Guinea-Bissau	28.1	0.1	17	23	82	0.4	37	5.8	0.2
Guyana	196.9	0.6	1,819	..	..	..	351	1.5	1.1
Haiti	27.6	0.4	7	0	1	3.4	50	3.3	0.1
Honduras	111.9	2.7	294	41	37	2.3	236	3.8	0.7
Hungary	92.3	113.5	660	17	19	-0.5	2,454	1.0	5.5
Iceland	100.3	0.1	636	..	..	..	7,996	2.6	6.7
India	2,973.2	20.5[c]	612	650	22	0.0	260	1.7	1.0
Indonesia	1,811.6	0.7	96	1,098	61	1.0	442	1.6	1.5
Iran, Islamic Rep.	1,622.0	54.6[c]	1,079	15	1	1.7	1,374	2.2	4.3
Iraq	437.4	121.6[c]	2,368	1	0	0.0	1,206	..	4.8
Ireland	68.9	1.7[c]	233	6	8	-2.7	3,196	4.4	9.0
Isle of Man	..	..	..	..	..	..	..	..	..
Israel	20.6	108.8	407	1	5	0.0	3,003	3.5	8.4
Italy	294.1	35.3	986	65	22	-0.1	2,821	5.4	7.2
Jamaica	10.8	3.9[c]	159	2	16	7.2	1,191	1.2	3.6
Japan	376.5	16.6	735	251	67	0.1	3,964	6.1	9.0
Jordan	88.9	66.2[c]	201	0	1	2.5	1,031	1.9	3.2
Kazakhstan	2,670.7	50.3	2,002	105	4	-1.9	3,337	0.3	13.3
Kenya	569.1	10.1	87	13	2	0.3	109	3.4	0.3
Kiribati	0.7	..	..	..	..	..	113	3.5	..
Korea, Dem. Rep.	120.4	21.1	727	62	51	0.0	1,113	..	11.6
Korea, Rep.	98.7	41.8	632	76	77	0.2	3,225	1.8	8.3
Kuwait	17.8	..	307	0	0	0.0	9,381	2.0	31.5
Kyrgyz Republic	191.8	23.4	2,257	7	4	0.0	513	0.5	1.2
Lao PDR	230.8	2.1	259	..	..	..	40	9.6	0.1
Latvia	62.1	4.2	114	29	46	-0.9	1,471	1.3	3.7
Lebanon	10.2	30.7[c]	444	1	5	7.8	1,120	1.3	3.3
Lesotho	30.4	1.0	30	0	0	0.0	..	..	..
Liberia	96.3	0.1	54	..	..	..	40	..	0.1
Libya	1,759.5	766.7	880	4	0	0.0	3,129	..	7.8
Liechtenstein	0.2	..	..	..	..	..	..	..	..

Economy	Land area thousand sq. km 1995	Annual water use[a] % of total water resources[b] 1980–96	Annual water use[a] Per capita cubic m 1980–96	Forest coverage Total area thousand sq. km 1995	Forest coverage As % of total land area 1995	Forest coverage Average annual deforestation % 1990–95	Energy use Per capita kg 1995	Energy use GDP per kilogram oil equivalent constant 1987 $ 1995	Carbon dioxide emissions per capita metric tons 1995
Lithuania	64.8	28.2	68	20	30	-0.6	2,291	0.8	4.0
Luxembourg	[d]	..	..	..	..	..	8,249	3.3	22.6
Macao	0.0	..	..	..	..	..	847	9.5	2.7
Macedonia, FYR	25.4	..	..	10	39	0.0	1,308	..	..
Madagascar	581.5	4.8	1,579	151	26	0.8	36	5.8	0.1
Malawi	94.1	5.1	98	33	35	1.6	38	3.8	0.1
Malaysia	328.6	2.1[c]	768	155	47	2.4	1,655	1.9	5.3
Maldives	0.3	..	..	..	..	..	141	5.0	0.7
Mali	1,220.2	2.3	162	116	9	1.0	21	12.1	0.0
Malta	0.3	..	..	..	..	..	2,261	3.1	4.7
Marshall Islands	..	..	..	..	..	..	..	..	..
Martinique	1.1	..	..	..	..	..	647	..	5.4
Mauritania	1,025.2	407.5[c]	923	6	1	0.0	102	5.0	1.3
Mauritius	2.0	16.4[c]	410	0	6	0.0	388	6.6	1.3
Mayotte	..	..	..	..	..	..	..	..	..
Mexico	1,908.7	21.7[c]	915	554	29	0.9	1,456	1.3	3.9
Micronesia, Fed. Sts.	..	..	..	..	..	..	..	..	..
Moldova	33.0	370.0	667	4	11	0.0	963	..	2.5
Monaco	..	..	..	..	..	..	..	..	..
Mongolia	1,566.5	2.2	271	94	6	0.0	1,045	..	3.4
Morocco	446.3	36.2	433	38	9	0.3	311	2.8	1.1
Mozambique	784.1	0.6	40	169	22	0.7	38	3.4	0.1
Myanmar	657.6	0.4	101	272	41	1.4	50	..	0.2
Namibia	823.3	4.0	179	124	15	0.3	..	..	..
Nepal	143.0	1.6	154	48	34	1.1	33	6.4	0.1
Netherlands	33.9	78.1	518	3	10	0.0	4,741	3.7	8.8
Netherlands Antilles	..	..	..	..	..	..	9,260	..	-0.1
New Caledonia	..	..	..	..	..	..	3,172	..	8.9
New Zealand	268.0	0.6	589	79	29	-0.6	4,290	2.7	7.6
Nicaragua	121.4	0.5[c]	368	56	46	2.5	265	3.1	0.6
Niger	1,266.7	14.3	69	26	2	0.0	37	7.5	0.1
Nigeria	910.8	1.6	41	138	15	0.9	165	1.9	0.8
Northern Mariana Islands	..	..	..	..	..	..	..	..	..
Norway	306.8	0.5	488	81	26	-0.2	5,439	4.7	16.6
Oman	212.5	123.2	656	0	0	..	1,880	3.1	5.3
Pakistan	770.9	62.7[c]	1,269	17	2	2.9	243	1.6	0.7
Palau	..	..	..	..	..	..	..	..	..
Panama	74.4	0.9	754	28	38	2.1	678	3.9	2.6
Papua New Guinea	452.9	0.0	28	369	82	0.4	232	4.6	0.6
Paraguay	397.3	0.5	112	115	29	2.6	308	3.4	0.8
Peru	1,280.0	15.3	300	676	53	0.3	421	0.7	1.3
Philippines	298.2	9.1[c]	686	68	23	3.5	307	2.0	0.9
Poland	304.4	24.9	321	87	29	-0.1	2,448	0.7	8.8
Portuga	91.5	19.2	738	29	31	-0.9	1,939	2.7	5.2
Puerto Rico	8.9	..	..	3	31	0.9	1,993	4.2	4.2
Qatar	11.0	..	..	..	..	..	12,248	..	45.2
Reunion	2.5	..	..	..	..	..	661	..	2.4
Romania	230.3	70.3	1,139	62	27	0.0	1,941	0.7	5.3
Russian Federation	16,888.5	2.7	521	7,635	45	0.0	4,079	0.5	12.3
Rwanda	24.7	12.2	135	3	10	0.2	33	6.3	0.1
Samoa	2.8	..	..	..	..	..	424	1.4	0.8
São Tomé and Principe	1.0	..	..	..	..	..	182	2.6	0.6
Saudi Arabia	2,149.7	709.2[c]	1,003	2	0	0.8	4,360	1.2	13.4
Senegal	192.5	5.2	202	74	38	0.7	104	6.1	0.4
Seychelles	0.5	..	..	..	..	..	1,633	2.8	..
Sierra Leone	71.6	0.2	98	13	18	3.0	72	2.2	0.1
Singapore	0.6	31.7[c]	84	0	7	0.0	7,162	2.0	21.3
Slovak Republic	48.1	5.8	337	20	41	-0.1	3,272	0.9	7.1
Slovenia	20.1	..	..	11	54	0.0	2,806	..	5.9
Solomon Islands	28.0	..	..	..	..	..	156	4.2	0.4
Somalia	627.3	13.5	99	..	..	..	7	..	0.0
South Africa	1,221.0	29.7	359	85	7	0.2	2,405	1.0	8.3
Spain	499.4	27.9	781	84	17	0.0	2,639	3.5	5.9
Sri Lanka	64.6	14.6[c]	503	18	28	1.1	136	3.8	0.3
St. Kitts and Nevis	0.4	..	..	..	..	..	512	7.6	..
St. Lucia	0.6	..	..	..	..	..	346	7.9	..
St. Vincent and the Grenadines	0.4	..	..	..	..	..	207	8.7	..
Sudan	2,376.0	50.9	666	416	18	0.8	65	12.1	0.1
Suriname	156.0	0.2	1,192	..	..	..	1,855	1.1	5.0
Swaziland	17.2	11.0	1,171	..	..	..	260	3.6	0.5
Sweden	411.6	1.7	340	244	59	0.0	5,736	3.4	5.0
Switzerland	39.6	2.8	173	11	29	0.0	3,571	7.5	5.5
Syrian Arab Republic	183.8	205.9	1,069	2	1	2.2	1,001	1.3	3.3
Tajikistan	140.6	19.0	2,001	4	3	0.0	563	0.5	0.6
Tanzania	883.6	1.5	40	325	37	1.0	32	..	0.1
Thailand	510.9	29.0	602	116	23	2.6	878	2.1	2.9
Togo	54.4	0.8	28	12	23	1.4	45	7.1	0.2
Tonga	0.7	..	..	..	..	..	196	4.7	..
Trinidad and Tobago	5.1	2.9[c]	148	2	31	1.5	5,381	0.7	13.3
Tunisia	155.4	87.2	376	6	4	0.5	591	2.4	1.7
Turkey	769.6	16.1	544	89	12	0.0	1,009	1.8	2.7
Turkmenistan	469.9	2,280.0	5,723	38	8	0.0	3,047	..	6.3
Uganda	199.7	0.5	20	61	31	0.9	22	24.8	0.1
Ukraine	579.4	65.3	504	92	16	-0.1	3,136	0.2	8.5
United Arab Emirates	83.6	1,406.7	954	1	1	0.0	11,567	..	27.8
United Kingdom	241.6	16.6	204	24	10	-0.5	3,786	3.5	9.3
United States	9,159.1	19.0	1,839	2,125	23	-0.3	7,905	2.6	20.8
Uruguay	174.8	1.1[c]	241	8	5	0.0	639	4.4	1.7
Uzbekistan	414.2	504.3	2,501	91	22	-2.7	2,043	0.3	4.3
Vanuatu	12.2	..	..	..	..	..	279	3.0	0.4
Venezuela	882.1	0.5[c]	382	440	50	1.1	2,158	1.2	8.3
Vietnam	325.5	7.7	416	91	28	1.4	104	7.8	0.4
Virgin Islands (U.S.)	0.3	..	..	..	..	..	34,303	..	..
West Bank and Gaza	..	..	..	..	..	..	..	..	..
Yemen, Rep.	528.0	71.5	253	0	0	0.0	192	..	..
Yugoslavia, FR (Serb./Mont.)	102.0	..	..	18	17	0.0	1,125	..	3.1
Zambia	743.4	2.1	216	314	42	0.8	145	1.7	0.3
Zimbabwe	386.9	8.7	136	87	23	0.6	424	1.4	0.9

.. Not available.

Note: Figures in italics are for years other than those specified; 0 or 0.0 means zero or less than half the unit shown and not known more precisely.

a. Data refer to any year from 1980 to 1996 unless otherwise noted and cover domestic, industrial, and agricultural uses. b. Data refer to internal renewable water resources. c. Data refer to years before 1980. d. Land area for Belgium includes Luxembourg.

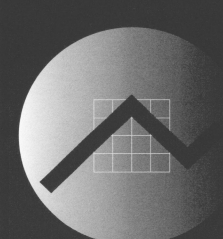

Economy

Developing countries set the pace for global economic growth over the past two decades, but the gap between leaders and laggards grew wider. While incomes rose in some of the most heavily populated countries, others experienced further deterioration in living standards, often as a result of political and social upheavals.

Developing economies with the strongest growth rates were generally characterized by:

- Commitment to better policies for macroeconomic management.
- Open-door policies toward foreign trade and foreign investment that contributed to closer integration with the global economy.
- Strong growth of the service sector and expanding trade in services.
- A decreasing share of central government spending in GDP.

Starting from a 30-year low of 2 percent in the early 1990s, the pace of global economic expansion returned to near 3 percent a year in 1996–97, a growth rate similar to that achieved during the 1980s. Developing countries (excluding Eastern Europe and the former Soviet Union) achieved GDP growth averaging more than 5 percent. Low- and middle-income economies in East Asia (including China) made the largest gains, averaging over 10 percent a year, though progress slackened in the mid-1990s because of flagging exports and, more recently, financial crisis. In South Asia growth accelerated to more than 6 percent in 1996 from 4.5 percent in the previous five years. In Latin America and the Caribbean and the Middle East and North Africa foreign trade has helped maintain growth rates of about 3 percent a year since 1991. Sub-Saharan Africa achieved growth of almost 4 percent in 1996, while the transition economies of Eastern Europe and the former Soviet Union began to arrest their decline.

Économie

Les pays en développement ont joué un rôle moteur dans la croissance économique mondiale au cours des deux dernières décennies, mais l'écart entre les plus performants et ceux restés à la traîne est allé croissant. Si certains des pays les plus peuplés ont enregistré une progression de leur revenu, d'autres ont vu leur niveau de vie se dégrader encore, souvent sous l'effet de troubles politiques et sociaux.

D'une manière générale, les pays en développement qui ont connu les plus forts taux de croissance se caractérisaient par :

• Une détermination à appliquer de meilleures politiques en matière de gestion macroéconomique.

• Des politiques d'ouverture au commerce extérieur et aux investissements étrangers, qui ont contribué à renforcer leur intégration à l'économie mondiale.

• Une forte progression du secteur des services, et un accroissement des échanges dans ce domaine.

• Une réduction de la part des dépenses de l'administration centrale dans le PIB.

De 2 % au début des années 90 (niveau le plus bas jamais atteint depuis 30 ans), l'expansion économique mondiale est repassée à un taux annuel de près de 3 % en 1996-97, soit un niveau analogue à celui des années 80. Dans les pays en développement (à l'exclusion des pays d'Europe de l'Est et de l'ex-Union soviétique), la croissance du PIB a dépassé 5 % en moyenne. C'est dans les pays à faible revenu et à revenu intermédiaire d'Asie de l'Est (y compris la Chine) que la croissance a été la plus soutenue, avec une moyenne de plus de 10 % par an, mais cette progression s'est ralentie au milieu des années 90 sous l'effet d'un fléchissement des exportations et, plus récemment, d'une crise financière. En Asie du Sud, le taux de croissance est passé à plus de 6 % en 1996, contre 4,5 % au cours des cinq années précédentes. Dans la région Amérique latine et Caraïbes et la région Moyen-Orient et Afrique du Nord, les échanges extérieurs ont contribué à maintenir les taux de croissance aux alentours de 3 % par an depuis 1991. L'Afrique subsaharienne, pour sa part, a connu une croissance de près de 4 % en 1996, tandis que les pays en transition d'Europe de l'Est et de l'ex-Union soviétique ont commencé à enrayer leur déclin.

Economía

Los países en desarrollo han marcado el ritmo del crecimiento económico mundial en los dos últimos decenios, pero al mismo tiempo se ha agrandado la diferencia entre los que ocupan los primeros puestos y los que van a la zaga. Aunque el ingreso ha aumentado en algunos de los países con mayor densidad de población, en otros se ha producido un deterioro del nivel de vida, debido en muchos casos a problemas de agitación política y social.

En general, los países en desarrollo que han registrado las tasas de crecimiento más altas han presentado las siguientes características:

• Empeño en mejorar las políticas relacionadas con la gestión macroeconómica.

• Políticas de puertas abiertas al comercio exterior y la inversión extranjera, que han contribuido a una integración más estrecha en la economía mundial.

• Robusto crecimiento del sector de servicios y expansión de su comercio.

• Descenso de la proporción del gasto del gobierno central con respecto al PIB.

Partiendo de un 2% —el nivel más bajo registrado en 30 años— a principios de los años noventa, el ritmo de expansión de la economía mundial volvió a situarse en casi un 3% anual en 1996–97, tasa de crecimiento similar a la de los años ochenta. Los países en desarrollo (excluidos los de Europa oriental y la antigua Unión Soviética) lograron aumentos del PIB de más del 5%. Las economías de ingreso bajo y mediano de Asia oriental (incluida China) fueron las que registraron aumentos más altos —con una media del 10% anual— aunque los avances perdieron impulso a mediados de los años noventa debido a la atonía de las exportaciones y, más recientemente, a la crisis financiera. En Asia meridional, se produjo una aceleración del crecimiento, que superó el 6% en 1996, frente al 4,5% de los cinco años anteriores. En América Latina y el Caribe y en Oriente Medio y Norte de África, el comercio exterior ha ayudado a mantener tasas de crecimiento de alrededor del 3% anual desde 1991. Los países de África al sur del Sahara registraron un crecimiento de casi el 4% en 1996, mientras que en las economías en transición de Europa oriental y la antigua Unión Soviética se ha empezado a frenar su descenso.

GNP per capita, 1996

Gross national product—the sum of gross value added by resident producers (plus taxes less subsidies) and net primary income from nonresident sources—divided by midyear population.

PNB par habitant, 1996

Produit national brut — somme de la valeur ajoutée brute par les producteurs résidents (majorée des taxes, minorée des subventions) et des montants nets de revenu primaire versés par des non-résidents — divisé par la population en milieu d'année.

PNB per cápita, 1996

Producto nacional bruto —suma del valor bruto agregado por todos los productores residentes (más los impuestos menos las subvenciones) más las entradas netas de ingreso primario de no residentes— dividido por la población de mediados de año.

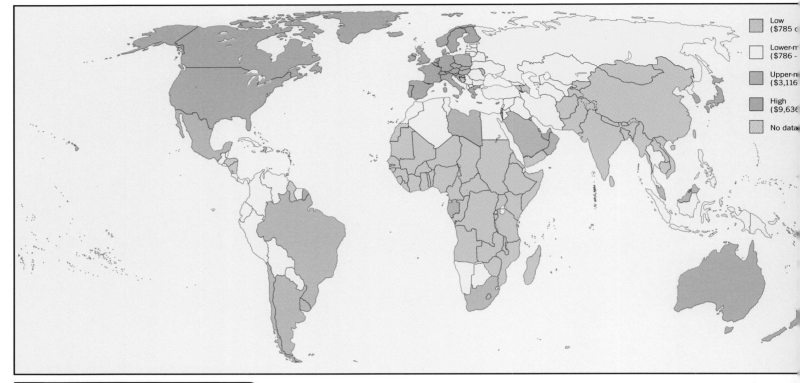

Low
($785 o

Lower-m
($786 -

Upper-m
($3,116

High
($9,636

No data

Distribution of world population among economies grouped by GNP per capita

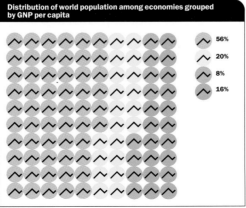

- 56%
- 20%
- 8%
- 16%

GNP per capita, 1996, $

East Asia & Pacific	890
Europe & Central Asia	2,200
Latin America & Caribbean	3,710
Middle East & N. Africa	2,070
South Asia	380
Sub-Saharan Africa	490
High income	25,870

0   5,000   10,000   15,000   20,000   25,000   30,000

GNP per capita, 1996, $

	Economies	GNP $ millions 1996	Population millions 1996	GNP per capita $ 1996
Low ($785 or less)	63	1,596,837	3,236	490
Lower–middle				
($786 to $3,115)	63	1,962,719	1,125	1,740
Upper–middle				
($3,116 to $9,635)	31	2,178,234	473	4,600
High				
($9,636 or more)	53	23,771,825	919	25,870
World	210	29,509,614	5,754	5,130

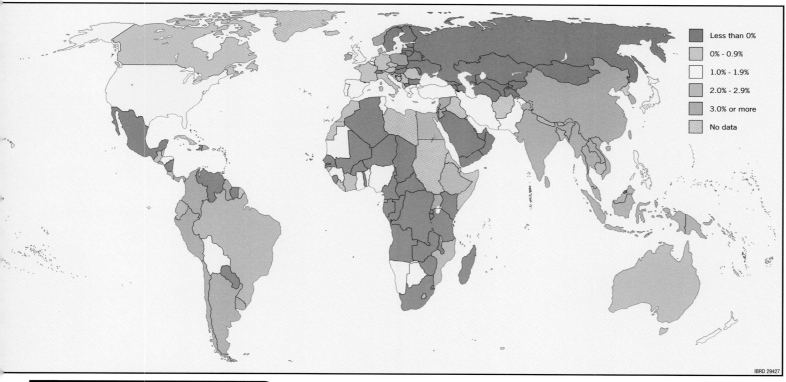

	Less than 0%
	0% - 0.9%
	1.0% - 1.9%
	2.0% - 2.9%
	3.0% or more
	No data

IBRD 29427

The average annual percentage change in a country's real GNP per capita. To exclude the effects of inflation, constant price GNP is used in calculating the growth rate.

Taux de croissance du PNB par habitant, 1990–96
Variation annuelle moyenne, en pourcentage, du PNB réel par habitant, calculée à partir du PNB en prix constants afin de faire abstraction des effets de l'inflation

Tasa de crecimiento del PNB per cápita, 1990–96
Variación porcentual anual media del PNB per cápita real de un país. A fin de excluir los efectos de la inflación, se utiliza el PNB medido en precios constantes para calcular la tasa de crecimiento.

Distribution of world population among economies grouped by GNP per capita growth rate

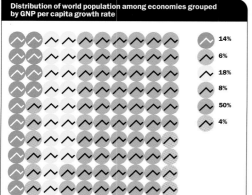

	14%
	6%
	18%
	8%
	50%
	4%

Index of GNP per capita, 1980–96, 1980 = 100

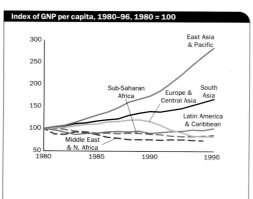

GNP per capita annual growth rate, 1990–96, percent

	Economies	GNP $ millions 1996	Population millions 1996	GNP per capita $ 1996
Less than 0%	69	2,152,165	832	2,590
0%–0.9%	21	6,037,894	342	17,680
1.0%–1.9%	25	15,772,567	1,043	15,130
2.0%–2.9%	20	1,399,561	488	2,870
3.0% or more	39	3,899,334	2,896	1,350
No data	36	248,094	153	1,620

Agriculture share in GDP, 1996

The value added in a country's agricultural sector as a percentage of gross domestic product.

Part de l'agriculture dans le PIB, 1996

Valeur ajoutée du secteur agricole en pourcentage du produit intérieur brut

Proporción de la agricultura en el PIB, 1996

Valor agregado en el sector agrícola de un país como porcentaje del producto interno bruto.

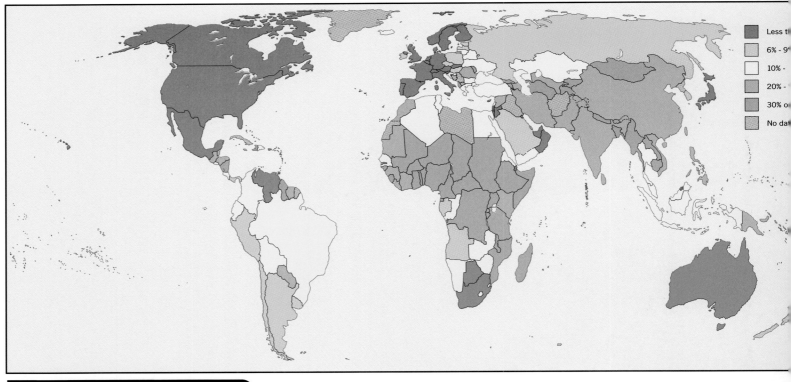

Less t	
6% - 9	
10% -	
20% -	
30% o	
No da	

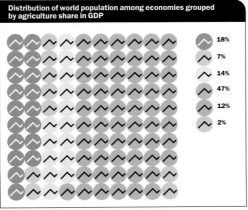

Distribution of world population among economies grouped by agriculture share in GDP

- 18%
- 7%
- 14%
- 47%
- 12%
- 2%

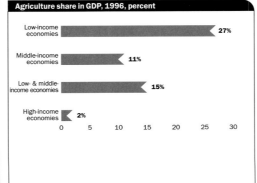

Agriculture share in GDP, 1996, percent

- Low-income economies — 27%
- Middle-income economies — 11%
- Low- & middle-income economies — 15%
- High-income economies — 2%

0 5 10 15 20 25 30

Agriculture share in GDP, 1996, percent

	Economies	GNP $ millions 1996	Population millions 1996	GNP per capita $ 1996
Less than 6%	43	23,631,889	1,027	23,010
6%–9%	20	1,786,497	378	4,730
10%–19%	37	1,945,440	839	2,320
20%–29%	28	1,745,517	2,697	650
30% or more	44	177,141	701	250
No data	38	223,131	112	2,000

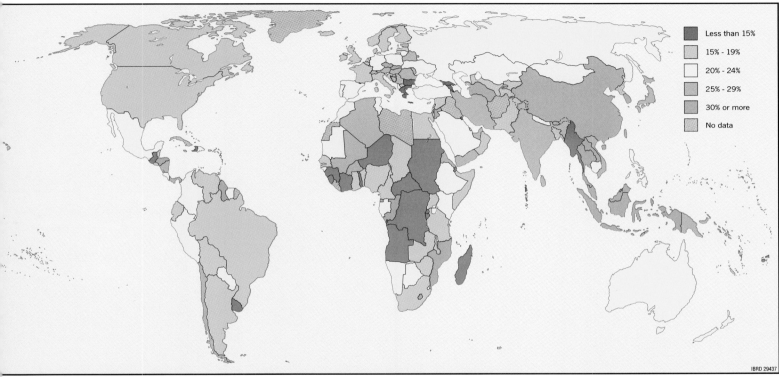

	Less than 15%
	15% - 19%
	20% - 24%
	25% - 29%
	30% or more
	No data

IBRD 29437

Outlays on additions to the fixed assets of an economy plus net changes in the level of inventories, as a percentage of gross domestic product.

Part de l'investissement dans le PIB, 1996

Dépenses consacrées à l'accroissement du capital fixe de l'économie, plus variations nettes du niveau des stocks, en pourcentage du produit intérieur brut.

Proporción de la inversión en el PIB, 1996

Desembolsos en concepto de adiciones a los activos fijos de la economía, más los cambios netos en el nivel de los inventarios, como porcentaje del producto interno bruto.

Distribution of world population among economies grouped by gross domestic investment as a share of GDP

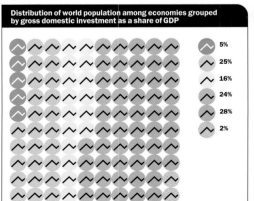

- 5%
- 25%
- 16%
- 24%
- 28%
- 2%

Gross domestic investment as a share of GDP in selected developing economies, 1996, percent

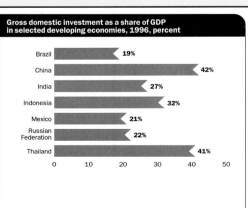

Economy	Percent
Brazil	19%
China	42%
India	27%
Indonesia	32%
Mexico	21%
Russian Federation	22%
Thailand	41%

(scale 0 10 20 30 40 50)

Investment share in GDP, 1996, percent

	Economies	GNP $ millions 1996	Population millions 1996	GNP per capita $ 1996
Less than 15%	24	259,913	252	1,030
15%–19%	49	14,827,985	1,442	10,280
20%–24%	41	5,436,948	943	5,770
25%–29%	28	6,225,321	1,387	4,490
30% or more	31	2,236,286	1,615	1,390
No data	37	523,161	116	4,520

Economy	GNP $ millions 1996[a]	GNP per capita $ 1996[a]	GNP per capita PPP[b] international $ 1996	GNP per capita Average annual real growth % 1990–96	Agriculture % of GDP 1996	Investment % of GDP 1996	Average annual inflation rate % 1990–96	Current account balance % of GDP 1996	Total external debt $ millions 1996
Afghanistan	..	.. c	..	..	..	..	..	..	..
Albania	2,705	820	..	2.2	55	21	67.9	–4.0	781
Algeria	43,726	1,520	4,620[d]	–1.9	13	27	25.4	..	33,260
American Samoa	..	.. e	..	..	..	..	..	..	..
Andorra	..	.. f	..	..	..	..	..	..	..
Angola	2,972	270	1,030	–5.6	7	11	1,103.2	–7.9	10,612
Antigua and Barbuda	482	7,330	8,660	2.0	4	47	2.6	–3.6	..
Argentina	295,131	8,380	9,530	3.9	6	19	15.8	–1.4	93,841
Armenia	2,387	630	2,160	–15.0	44	10	896.6	–19.2	552
Aruba	..	.. f	..	2.4	..	..	4.5	6.6	..
Australia	367,802	20,090	19,870	2.7	4	21	1.1	–4.0	..
Austria	226,510	28,110	21,650	0.9	2	25	3.0	–1.9	..
Azerbaijan	3,642	480	1,490	–18.7	23	24	589.9	–18.2	435
Bahamas, The	..	.. f	10,180	–2.0	..	..	2.9	–4.2	..
Bahrain	..	.. e	13,970	3.8	1	27	–0.5	11.0	..
Bangladesh	31,217	260	1,010	2.7	30	17	4.9	–5.1	16,083
Barbados	..	.. e	10,510	–0.8	5	13	0.7	5.2	581
Belarus	22,452	2,070	4,380	–8.6	16	25	714.9	–4.7	1,071
Belgium	268,633	26,440	22,390	1.2	1	18	2.8	5.4	..
Belize	600	2,700	4,170	0.7	21	19	3.9	–2.9	288
Benin	1,998	350	1,230	1.9	38	17	10.8	2.4	1,594
Bermuda	..	.. f	..	..	..	..	..	..	..
Bhutan	282	390	..	2.0	42	47	9.3	–15.0	87
Bolivia	6,302	830	2,860	1.8	§	15	10.5	–4.9	5,174
Bosnia and Herzegovina	..	.. c	..	..	..	..	..	..	815
Botswana	..	.. g	7,390	1.3	4	24	9.7	7.5	613
Brazil	709,591	4,400	6,340	2.0	14	19	675.4	–3.2	179,047
Brunei	..	.. f	..	–1.5	§	..	0.0	..	..
Bulgaria	9,924	1,190	4,280	–1.8	10	14	80.3	–0.2	9,819
Burkina Faso	2,410	230	950[d]	–0.1	35	25	7.1	0.8	1,294
Burundi	1,066	170	590	–6.4	57	9	14.3	–0.5	1,127
Cambodia	3,088	300	..	2.9	51	21	44.7	–9.5	2,111
Cameroon	8,356	610	1,760	–3.8	40	16	6.4	–2.4	9,515
Canada	569,899	19,020	21,380	0.6	§	18	1.3	0.5	..
Cape Verde	393	1,010	2,640[d]	–16.7	7	34	3.6	–9.2	211
Cayman Islands	..	.. f	..	..	..	..	..	..	..
Central African Republic	1,024	310	1,430[d]	–1.7	56	6	6.6	–2.7	928
Chad	1,035	160	880[d]	–1.7	46	19	8.6	–4.5	997
Channel Islands	..	.. f	..	..	..	..	..	..	..
Chile	70,060	4,860	11,700	6.4	§	28	13.6	–3.9	27,411
China	906,079	750	3,330	11.0	21	42	12.0	0.9	128,817
Hong Kong, China[h]	153,288	24,290	24,260	3.7	0	32	7.0	..	..
Colombia	80,174	2,140	6,720	3.0	16	21	23.0	–5.6	28,859
Comoros	228	450	1,770[d]	–1.8	40	17	4.4	–8.1	206
Congo, Dem. Rep.	5,727	130	790[d]	–10.4	64	6	2,746.5	..	12,826
Congo, Rep.	1,813	670	1,410	–4.3	10	61	8.3	–43.3	5,240
Costa Rica	9,081	2,640	6,470	2.4	16	23	18.4	–1.6	3,454
Côte d'Ivoire	9,434	660	1,580	0.2	28	14	9.8	–1.9	19,713
Croatia	18,130	3,800	4,290	2.2	12	15	218.1	–7.6	4,634
Cuba	..	.. g	..	..	..	..	..	..	..
Cyprus	..	.. f	20,490[d]	2.6	5	22	4.3	1.0	..
Czech Republic	48,861	4,740	10,870	0.9	6	35	17.7	–7.8	20,094
Denmark	168,917	32,100	22,120	2.1	§	17	1.8	1.1	..
Djibouti	..	.. g	..	..	3	9	4.9	–4.7	241
Dominica	228	3,090	4,390	2.3	20	27	..	–16.4	110
Dominican Republic	12,765	1,600	4,390	3.1	13	24	12.3	–0.8	4,310
Ecuador	17,531	1,500	4,730	0.8	12	17	35.0	1.5	14,491
Egypt, Arab Rep.	64,275	1,080	2,860	2.2	17	17	11.3	0.7	31,407
El Salvador	9,868	1,700	2,790	3.5	13	16	10.8	–3.4	2,894
Equatorial Guinea	217	530	2,690	15.9	34	114	3.9	–120.6	283
Eritrea	..	.. c	..	..	10	26	16.1	..	46
Estonia	4,509	3,080	4,660	–4.9	7	27	116.7	–10.3	405
Ethiopia	6,042	100	500	2.0	55	21	9.7	–7.7	10,077
Faeroe Islands	..	.. f	..	..	..	..	..	..	..
Fiji	1,983	2,470	4,070	0.6	23	14	3.3	0.5	217
Finland	119,086	23,240	18,260	–0.2	§	16	1.8	3.9	..
France	1,533,619	26,270	21,510	0.7	2	18	2.0	1.3	..
French Guiana	..	.. f	..	..	..	..	..	..	..
French Polynesia	..	.. f	..	..	..	..	..	..	..
Gabon	4,444	3,950	6,300	–1.2	7	20	9.8	1.9	4,213
Gambia, The	..	.. c	1,280[d]	–0.5	28	21	5.4	–2.3	452
Georgia	4,590	850	1,810	–19.3	35	4	2,279.3	–5.0	1,356
Germany	2,364,632	28,870	21,110	0.7	1	23	2.9	–0.6	..
Ghana	6,223	360	1,790[d]	1.5	44	19	26.9	–5.1	6,202
Greece	120,021	11,460	12,730	1.3	§	14	12.2	–3.7	..
Greenland	..	.. f	..	..	..	..	..	..	..
Grenada	285	2,880	4,340	0.6	11	32	2.3	–12.7	120
Guadeloupe	..	.. f	..	..	..	..	..	..	..
Guam	..	.. f	..	..	..	..	..	..	..
Guatemala	16,018	1,470	3,820	0.5	24	13	13.0	–2.9	3,785
Guinea	3,804	560	1,720	1.9	26	13	8.8	–4.5	3,240
Guinea-Bissau	270	250	1,030	0.5	54	22	47.8	–10.2	937
Guyana	582	690	2,280	10.4	36	30	26.4	–21.7	1,631
Haiti	2,282	310	1,130[d]	–6.9	42	2	25.0	–5.3	897
Honduras	4,012	660	2,130	1.2	22	32	20.0	–5.1	4,453
Hungary	44,274	4,340	6,730	–0.6	7	27	22.5	–3.8	26,958
Iceland	7,175	26,580	21,710	0.5	§	15	3.1	0.7	..
India	357,759	380	1,580	3.8	28	27	9.2	–1.1	89,827
Indonesia	213,384	1,080	3,310	5.9	16	32	8.1	–3.7	129,033
Iran, Islamic Rep.	..	.. g	5,360	1.0	25	29	32.3	..	21,183
Iraq	..	.. g	..	..	..	..	..	..	..
Ireland	62,040	17,110	16,750	5.1	§	15	1.9	2.0	..
Isle of Man	.. i	.. e	..	..	..	..	..	..	..
Israel	90,310	15,870	18,100	3.2	§	24	12.2	–5.7	..
Italy	1,140,484	19,880	19,890	0.9	3	18	4.7	3.4	..
Jamaica	4,066	1,600	3,450	0.9	8	27	36.1	–1.9	4,041
Japan	5,149,185	40,940	23,420	1.2	2	29	0.7	1.4	..
Jordan	7,088	1,650	3,570	4.0	5	35	4.0	–3.1	8,118
Kazakhstan	22,213	1,350	3,230	–10.3	13	23	604.9	–3.6	2,920
Kenya	8,661	320	1,130	–0.5	29	20	16.6	–0.8	6,893
Kiribati	75	920	..	–0.6	§	§	6.4	3.6	..
Korea, Dem. Rep.	..	.. g	..	..	..	..	..	..	..
Korea, Rep.	483,130	10,610	13,080	6.2	6	38	5.8	–4.8	..
Kuwait	..	.. f	.. d	15.7	0	12	..	17.2	..
Kyrgyz Republic	2,486	550	1,970	–12.7	52	19	256.2	–23.0	789
Lao PDR	1,895	400	1,250	3.9	52	31	11.1	–6.9	2,263
Latvia	5,730	2,300	3,650	–10.1	9	19	110.6	–8.3	472
Lebanon	12,118	2,970	6,060	5.4	12	30	32.8	–25.7	3,996
Lesotho	1,331	660	2,380[d]	0.9	11	104	8.8	14.1	654
Liberia	..	.. c	..	..	..	..	..	..	2,107
Libya	..	.. e	..	..	..	..	..	..	..
Liechtenstein	..	.. f	..	..	..	..	..	..	..

Economy	GNP $ millions 1996a	GNP per capita $ 1996a	GNP per capita PPPb international $ 1996	Average annual real growth % 1990–96	Agriculture % of GDP 1996	Investment % of GDP 1996	Average annual inflation rate % 1990–96	Current account balance % of GDP 1996	Total external debt $ millions 1996
Lithuania	8,455	2,280	4,390	−6.0	13	21	179.3	−9.3	1,286
Luxembourg	18,850	45,360	34,480	0.1	*1*	§	2.6	..	..
Macao	..	..f	..	..	..	31	9.6	..	..
Macedonia, FYR	1,956	990	..	−8.5	..	15	286.4	−13.9	1,659
Madagascar	3,428	250	900	−2.0	35	10	25.4	−3.7	4,175
Malawi	1,832	180	690	−0.2	40	17	33.2	−34.9	2,312
Malaysia	89,800	4,370	10,390	6.1	13	41	4.4	−8.6	39,777
Maldives	277	1,080	3,140	4.1	..	..	9.9	3.0	167
Mali	2,422	240	710	−0.2	48	27	10.6	−8.9	3,020
Malta	..	..e	13,870	*3.1*	§	§	*3.6*	−11.3	953
Marshall Islands	108	1,890	..	−4.0	§	..	6.4	..	..
Martinique	..	..f	..	..	..	..	..	..	..
Mauritania	1,089	470	1,810	1.7	25	22	6.2	*2.1*	2,363
Mauritius	4,205	3,710	9,000	3.6	10	26	6.5	0.4	1,818
Mayotte	..	..e	..	..	..	..	..	..	..
Mexico	341,718	3,670	7,660	−0.3	5	21	18.5	−0.6	157,125
Micronesia, Fed. Sts.	225	2,070	..	−1.3	..	..	4.7	..	..
Moldova	2,542	590	1,440	−16.8	50	28	307.7	−16.6	834
Monaco	..	..f	..	..	..	..	..	..	..
Mongolia	902	360	1,820	−2.3	31	22	106.2	*4.1*	524
Morocco	34,936	1,290	3,320	0.2	20	21	4.0	−1.7	21,767
Mozambique	1,472	80	500d	2.6	37	48	47.2	−30.4	5,842
Myanmar	..	..c	..	3.9	60	11	21.9	..	5,184
Namibia	3,569	2,250	5,390d	1.6	14	20	9.6	2.6	..
Nepal	4,710	210	1,090	2.3	42	23	10.1	−12.8	2,414
Netherlands	402,565	25,940	20,850	1.8	*3*	*19*	1.9	5.2	..
Netherlands Antilles	..	..f	..	..	..	..	..	..	..
New Caledonia	..	..f	..	..	..	..	..	..	..
New Zealand	57,135	15,720	16,500	1.7	§	*22*	1.8	−6.1	..
Nicaragua	1,705	380	1,760d	−0.2	34	28	70.9	−22.1	5,929
Niger	1,879	200	920d	−2.3	39	10	7.4	*−8.1*	1,557
Nigeria	27,599	240	870	1.2	43	19	37.6	9.7	31,407
Northern Mariana Islands	..	..f	..	..	..	..	..	..	..
Norway	151,198	34,510	23,220	3.7	*2*	§	1.7	7.1	..
Oman	..	..e	8,680	*−0.3*	§	17	−2.9	−6.6	3,415
Pakistan	63,567	480	1,600	1.1	26	19	11.3	−6.5	29,901
Palau	..	..e	..	..	..	..	..	..	..
Panama	8,249	3,080	7,060	3.6	8	29	2.7	−0.7	6,990
Papua New Guinea	5,049	1,150	2,820d	5.0	26	27	6.6	6.1	2,359
Paraguay	9,179	1,850	3,480	−1.5	24	23	17.4	−6.9	2,141
Peru	58,671	2,420	4,410	4.8	7	24	49.1	−5.9	29,176
Philippines	83,298	1,160	3,550	1.0	21	24	9.0	−4.5	41,214
Poland	124,682	3,230	6,000	3.3	*6*	20	32.4	−2.4	40,895
Portugal	100,934	10,160	13,450	1.5	§	§	7.0	−2.6	..
Puerto Rico	..	..e	..	..	§	§	..	..	..
Qatar	..	..f	16,330	−5.1	..	..	..	..	..
Reunion	..	..f	..	..	..	§	..	..	..
Romania	36,191	1,600	4,580	0.1	*21*	25	132.7	−7.2	8,291
Russian Federation	356,030	2,410	4,190	−9.2	*7*	22	394.0	2.6	124,785
Rwanda	1,268	190	630	−8.2	40	14	19.5	0.1	1,034
Samoa	200	1,170	..	0.1	§	§	2.2	7.0	167
São Tomé and Principe	45	330	..	−1.7	20	50	52.5	−75.5	261
Saudi Arabia	..	..e	9,700	*−3.1*	§	*20*	1.1	−4.3	..
Senegal	4,856	570	1,650	−0.6	18	17	8.4	*−1.2*	3,663
Seychelles	526	6,850	..	1.5	4	23	2.4	−3.9	148
Sierra Leone	925	200	510	−3.9	44	9	37.7	−9.6	1,167
Singapore	92,987	30,550	26,910	6.6	0	35	3.4	15.2	..
Slovak Republic	18,206	3,410	7,460	−1.2	5	38	14.2	−11.0	7,704
Slovenia	18,390	9,240	12,110	*4.4*	5	23	*39.2*	0.2	4,031
Solomon Islands	349	900	2,250d	1.3	§	§	11.3	..	145
Somalia	..	..c	..	..	§	§	..	..	2,643
South Africa	132,455	3,520	7,450d	−0.2	5	18	10.6	−1.6	23,590
Spain	563,249	14,350	15,290	1.0	*3*	*21*	5.0	0.3	..
Sri Lanka	13,475	740	2,290	3.4	22	25	10.4	−4.7	7,995
St. Kitts and Nevis	240	5,870	7,310	3.5	6	46	*4.0*	−11.9	58
St. Lucia	553	3,500	4,920	2.8	11	19	*3.1*	−12.5	142
St. Vincent and the Grenadines	264	2,370	4,160	2.4	*13*	30	*2.7*	−7.2	213
Sudan	..	..c	..	..	§	§	86.2	..	16,972
Suriname	433	1,000	2,630	−0.3	§	§	*138.1*	21.8	..
Swaziland	1,122	1,210	3,320	−1.2	12	21	10.6	0.9	220
Sweden	227,315	25,710	18,770	−0.2	§	*15*	2.8	2.4	..
Switzerland	313,729	44,350	26,340	−1.0	§	..	2.3	7.0	..
Syrian Arab Republic	16,808	1,160	3,020	4.3	§	§	*8.5*	2.2	21,420
Tajikistan	1,964	340	900	−18.5	§	*17*	394.3	−4.1	707
Tanzaniai	5,174	170	..	−0.2	48	18	25.9	−15.8	7,412
Thailand	177,476	2,960	6,700	6.7	11	41	4.8	−7.9	90,824
Togo	1,278	300	1,650	−3.9	35	14	9.4	*−6.1*	1,463
Tonga	175	1,790	..	2.0	37	§	3.7	..	70
Trinidad and Tobago	5,017	3,870	6,100	0.1	2	15	6.5	1.7	2,242
Tunisia	17,581	1,930	4,550	1.3	14	24	5.1	−2.7	9,887
Turkey	177,530	2,830	6,060	1.7	17	24	78.2	−0.8	79,789
Turkmenistan	4,319	940	2,010	−13.1	§	§	1,074.2	1.0	825
Uganda	5,826	300	1,030d	4.0	46	16	20.4	−8.2	3,674
Ukraine	60,904	1,200	2,230	−13.5	13	23	800.5	−2.3	9,335
United Arab Emirates	..	..f	17,000d	−4.8	§	27	..	..	..
United Kingdom	1,152,136	19,600	19,960	1.5	§	§	3.3	0.0	..
United States	7,433,517	28,020	28,020	1.2	§	*18*	2.5	−2.0	..
Uruguay	18,464	5,760	7,760	3.8	9	12	49.8	−1.6	5,899
Uzbekistan	23,490	1,010	2,450	−5.6	26	16	546.5	−4.3	2,319
Vanuatu	224	1,290	3,020d	−1.1	§	§	3.2	−9.1	47
Venezuela	67,333	3,020	8,130	−0.3	4	17	46.7	13.1	35,344
Vietnam	21,915	290	1,570	6.2	27	28	22.7	−11.3	26,764
Virgin Islands (U.S.)	..	..f	..	..	..	..	..	..	..
West Bank and Gaza	..	..g	..	..	..	..	..	..	..
Yemen, Rep.	6,016	380	790	−2.2	18	25	27.1	−1.2	6,356
Yugoslavia, FR (Serb./Mont.)	..	..g	..	..	..	..	..	..	13,439
Zambia	3,363	360	860	−4.8	18	15	86.8	..	7,113
Zimbabwe	6,815	610	2,200	−1.1	14	18	26.4	−2.1	5,005

.. Not available.
§ See map for range estimate.
Note: Figures in italics are for years other than those specified; 0 or 0.0 means zero or less than half the unit shown and not known more precisely.

a. Calculated using the Atlas method. b. Purchasing power parity; see the technical notes. c. Estimated to be low income ($785 or less). d. Estimate is based on regression; others are extrapolated from the 1993 International Comparison Programme survey. e. Estimated to be upper middle income ($3,116 to $9,635). f. Estimated to be high income ($9,636 or more). g. Estimated to be lower middle income ($786 to $3,115). h. Data for GNP are GDP. i. Data refer to mainland Tanzania only.

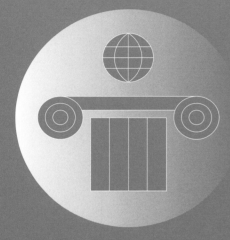

States and Markets

The state grew everywhere in the 20th century—but in very different ways, dictated by two world wars, the Russian revolution, the 1930s' depression, and decolonization. The diversity of experience makes it difficult to draw conclusions about what makes states and markets effective—and what size state is right for any set of social and economic circumstances.

In 1996 ratios of central government spending to gross domestic product ranged from less than 10 percent to about 50 percent. Different types of governments are looking for ways to freeze and eventually cut this spending without losing votes. Many developing country governments are shifting their priorities from preserving jobs in a stagnant public sector to creating jobs in a vibrant private sector. This shift implies a fundamental change in the role of government—from owner and operator to policymaker and regulator, working closely with the private sector to develop a competitive, outward-looking economy. The market is often the most acceptable and efficient solution—with private health and unemployment insurance, private contributions to education costs and care for the elderly, and even private prison services among reforms initiated in the 1990s.

The poorest countries lack many of the prerequisites for such a sustained effort—and have little latitude for error. The challenges are particularly daunting in Africa, where the business environment for entrepreneurs is shaky, markets are small, skills are shallow and narrow, the supporting infrastructure is weak, and laws and regulations are very restrictive.

The challenge for developing countries is to provide as good an institutional framework for development as their capabilities will allow. Governments should not intervene where markets can operate more efficiently, but governments should ensure that the rules of the market and the laws of the state are applied fairly and equitably to all.

État et Marché

Le XXe siècle a vu l'État se développer dans tous les pays mais de différentes manières, sous l'effet de deux guerres mondiales, de la Révolution russe, de la dépression des années 30 et de la décolonisation. Cette diversité fait qu'il est difficile de tirer des conclusions sur ce qui contribue à l'efficacité du marché et de l'État, et sur ce qui constitue la taille optimale de l'État dans un contexte économique et social donné.

En 1996, la part des dépenses de l'administration centrale dans le produit intérieur brut des pays s'est établie dans une fourchette de moins de 10 % à environ 50 %. Divers types de gouvernements recherchent aujourd'hui les moyens de geler et, à terme, de réduire ces dépenses sans pour autant perdre l'appui de leurs électeurs.

Dans beaucoup de pays en développement, l'axe prioritaire des gouvernements, à l'heure actuelle, consiste non plus à préserver des emplois dans un secteur public en stagnation, mais à en créer au niveau d'un secteur privé en plein essor. Cette évolution suppose un changement fondamental du rôle de l'État : au lieu de contrôler et de faire fonctionner l'économie, celui-ci doit jouer un rôle de décideur et de régulateur, travaillant en étroite coopération avec le secteur privé pour établir une économie ouverte et concurrentielle. Dans bien des cas, le marché représente la solution la plus acceptable et la plus rationnelle ; parmi les réformes engagées dans les années 90 figurent ainsi la mise en place de régimes d'assurance maladie et d'assurance chômage privés, la contribution du secteur privé aux dépenses d'éducation et aux soins en faveur des personnes âgées, voire l'instauration de services pénitentiaires privés.

Pour les pays les plus pauvres, une bonne partie des conditions préalables à un processus soutenu de ce type font défaut, et il n'y a guère de droit à l'erreur. Les défis sont particulièrement redoutables en Afrique, où le climat des affaires est peu propice aux entrepreneurs, les marchés sont peu développés, les compétences sont limitées, l'infrastructure d'appui est insuffisante et les lois et règlements sont très restrictifs.

Pour les pays en développement, le problème consiste à instituer le cadre institutionnel le plus propice au développement que permettront leurs capacités. Dans ces pays, l'État ne doit pas intervenir dans les domaines où les marchés peuvent opérer avec plus d'efficacité, mais les dirigeants doivent veiller à ce que les lois du marché et les règles de l'État s'appliquent de manière juste et équitable à tous.

Estados y Mercados

A lo largo del Siglo XX, las dimensiones del Estado han aumentado en todo el mundo, aunque en forma muy diferente, como consecuencia de dos guerras mundiales, la Revolución rusa, la depresión de los años treinta, y el proceso de descolonización. Dada esa diversidad de experiencias, es difícil saber cuáles son los factores en los que radica la eficiencia del Estado y de los mercados, y cuáles han de ser las dimensiones ideales del Estado para un conjunto dado de circunstancias sociales y económicas.

En 1996, la proporción entre el gasto del gobierno central y el producto interno bruto osciló entre menos del 10% y algo más del 50%. Los distintos gobiernos tratan de encontrar fórmulas para congelar y, en última instancia, reducir este gasto sin perder votos.

Muchos gobiernos de países en desarrollo están reorientando sus prioridades hacia la creación de empleo en un sector privado en auge en detrimento del mantenimiento del empleo en un sector público estancado. Esta reorientación conlleva un cambio radical en la función del Estado, que deja de ser el dueño y operador para convertirse en un agente que formula políticas y en un ente normativo, que colabora estrechamente con el sector privado para desarrollar una economía competitiva y orientada al exterior. Con frecuencia, el mercado es la solución más aceptable y eficiente, mereciendo destacar entre las reformas emprendidas en los años noventa la privatización de la atención de la salud y el seguro de desempleo, las contribuciones privadas para financiar los costos de la educación y la atención de la tercera edad, e incluso la privatización de las cárceles.

Los países más pobres carecen de muchos de los requisitos necesarios para realizar un esfuerzo sostenido de esta naturaleza, y tienen muy poco margen de error. La situación es especialmente desalentadora en África, donde las condiciones son poco propicias para la inversión, los mercados son pequeños, los conocimientos superficiales y poco diversificados, la infraestructura de apoyo débil y las leyes y reglamentos muy restrictivos.

El desafío que se presenta a los países en desarrollo es crear un marco institucional propicio en la medida de sus posibilidades. El Estado no debe intervenir cuando los mercados puedan operar en forma más eficiente; lo que debe hacer es velar por que los principios del mercado y las reglas del Estado se apliquen a todos por igual, con justicia y equidad.

Military expenditure share in GNP, 1995

Expenditures on military-related spending of the defense ministry, including recruiting, training, construction, and the purchase of military supplies and equipment, but excluding spending on public order and safety, as a percentage of gross national product.

Part des dépenses militaires dans le PNB, 1995

Dépenses à caractère militaire du ministère de la défense, y compris les opérations de recrutement, les activités de formation, les travaux de construction et l'achat de matériel et de fournitures militaires, mais à l'exclusion des dépenses destinées à la sécurité et à l'ordre public, en pourcentage du produit national brut.

Proporción del gasto militar en el PNB, 1995

El gasto militar del ministerio de defensa, incluidos el reclutamiento, el adiestramiento, la construcción y la adquisición de equipo y suministros militares, pero excluidos los gastos en seguridad y orden públicos, como porcentaje del producto nacional bruto.

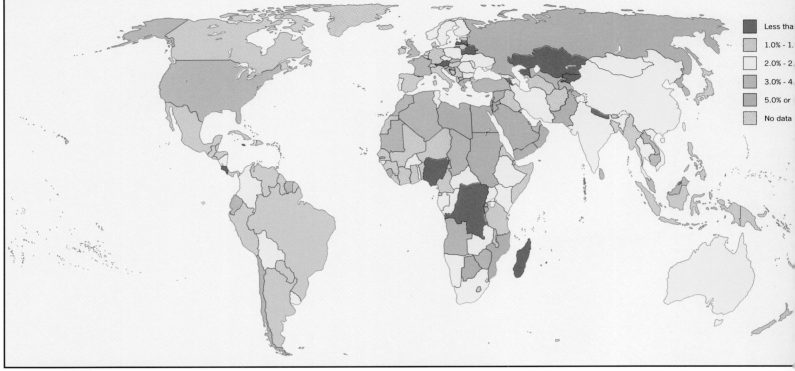

Less tha

1.0% - 1.

2.0% - 2

3.0% - 4

5.0% or

No data

Distribution of world population among economies grouped by military expenditure

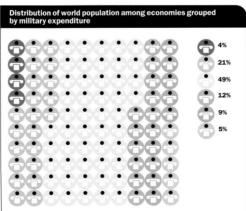

4%
21%
49%
12%
9%
5%

Military expenditure as a share of GNP in selected countries, 1995, percent

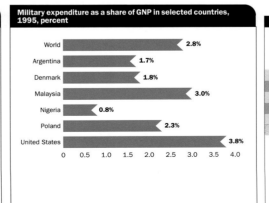

World	2.8%
Argentina	1.7%
Denmark	1.8%
Malaysia	3.0%
Nigeria	0.8%
Poland	2.3%
United States	3.8%

Military expenditure, 1995, percentage of GNP

	Economies	GNP $ millions 1996	Population millions 1996	GNP per capita $ 1996
Less than 1.0%	16	369,737	253	1,460
1.0%–1.9%	47	10,298,994	1,203	8,560
2.0%–2.9%	39	3,546,293	2,818	1,260
3.0%–4.9%	29	11,274,090	713	15,810
5.0% or more	22	1,008,626	507	1,990
No data	57	3,011,874	260	11,570

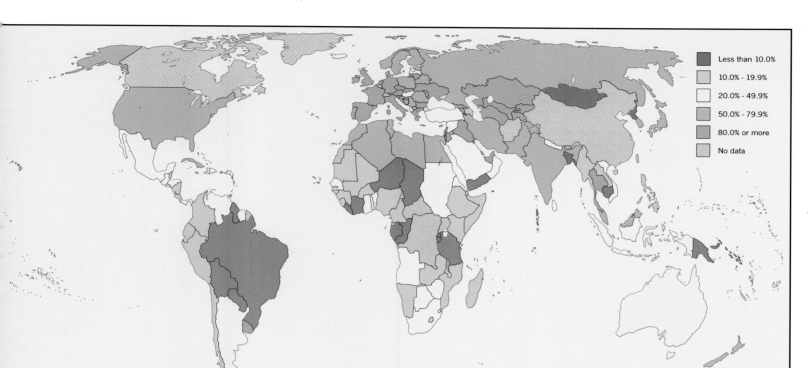

■	Less than 10.0%
▨	10.0% - 19.9%
□	20.0% - 49.9%
▦	50.0% - 79.9%
▨	80.0% or more
▨	No data

IBRD 29443

Roads that have been sealed with asphalt or similar road-building materials, as a percentage of total roads.

Part des routes revêtues dans le réseau routier total, 1996
Routes revêtues d'asphalte ou de matériaux analogues, en pourcentage du réseau routier total.

Carreteras pavimentadas como porcentaje del total de caminos, 1996
Carreteras que han sido cubiertas con asfalto u otros materiales similares para la construcción de caminos, como porcentaje del total de carreteras.

Distribution of world population among economies grouped by paved roads as percentage of total

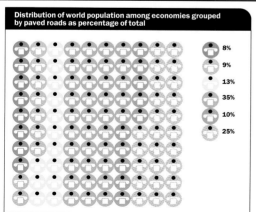

- 8%
- 9%
- 13%
- 35%
- 10%
- 25%

Paved roads as a percentage of total roads, 1996

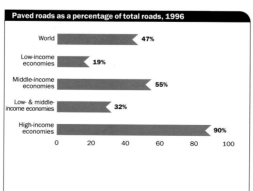

World	47%
Low-income economies	19%
Middle-income economies	55%
Low- & middle-income economies	32%
High-income economies	90%

0 20 40 60 80 100

Paved roads as a percentage of total roads, 1996

	Economies	GNP $ millions 1996	Population millions 1996	GNP per capita $ 1996
Less than 10.0%	21	819,626	433	1,890
10.0%–19.9%	30	348,292	491	710
20.0%–49.9%	41	1,948,821	764	2,550
50.0%–79.9%	37	15,061,716	2,006	7,510
80.0% or more	44	9,119,905	642	14,200
No data	37	2,211,255	1,417	1,560

Telephone mainlines per 1,000 people, 1996

Telephone lines connecting a customer's equipment to the public switched telephone network, per 1,000 people.

Lignes téléphoniques principales pour 1 000 habitants, 1996
Lignes téléphoniques raccordant le matériel d'un abonné au réseau téléphonique public commuté, pour 1 000 habitants.

Líneas telefónicas principales por cada 1.000 personas, 1996
Líneas telefónicas que conectan el equipo del cliente a la red telefónica pública conmutada, por cada 1.000 personas.

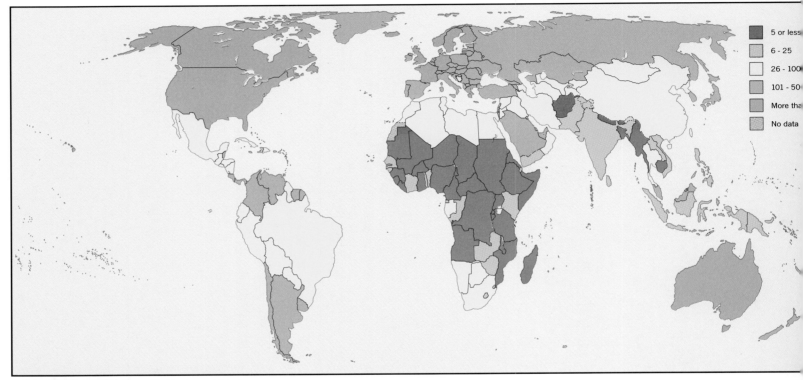

5 or less	
6 - 25	
26 - 100	
101 - 50	
More tha	
No data	

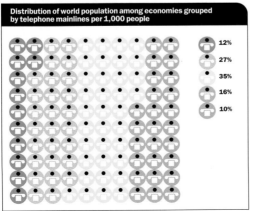

Distribution of world population among economies grouped by telephone mainlines per 1,000 people

- 12%
- 27%
- 35%
- 16%
- 10%

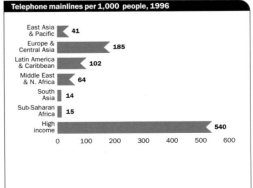

Telephone mainlines per 1,000 people, 1996

- East Asia & Pacific: 41
- Europe & Central Asia: 185
- Latin America & Caribbean: 102
- Middle East & N. Africa: 64
- South Asia: 14
- Sub-Saharan Africa: 15
- High income: 540

0 100 200 300 400 500 600

Telephone mainlines per 1,000 people, 1996

	Economies	GNP $ millions 1996	Population millions 1996	GNP per capita $ 1996
5 or less	32	160,715	688	230
6–25	28	813,992	1,567	520
26–100	47	2,906,912	1,981	1,470
101–500	78	10,420,769	938	11,110
More than 500	19	15,200,407	580	26,230
No data	6	6,819	0	18,190

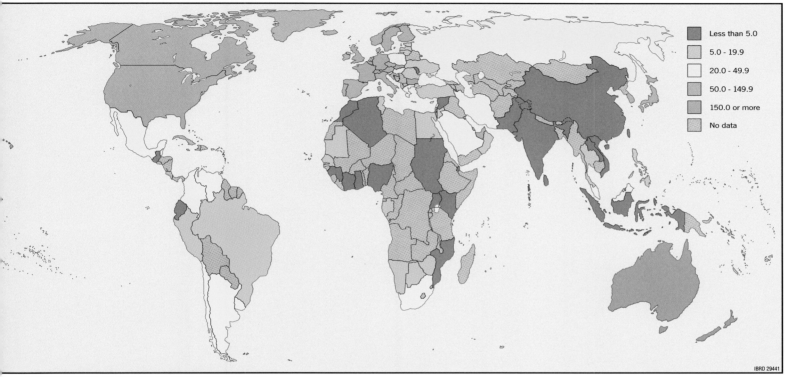

■	Less than 5.0
▦	5.0 - 19.9
□	20.0 - 49.9
▨	50.0 - 149.9
▨	150.0 or more
▨	No data

IBRD 29441

The estimated number of self-contained computers designed to be used by a single individual, per 1,000 people.

Ordinateurs individuels pour 1 000 habitants, 1996
Nombre estimatif d'ordinateurs destinés à l'usage individuel, pour 1 000 habitants.

Computadoras personales por cada 1.000 personas, 1996
Número estimado de computadoras autónomas destinadas al uso individual, por cada 1.000 personas.

Distribution of world population among economies grouped by personal computers per 1,000 people

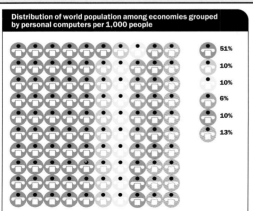

- 51%
- 10%
- 10%
- 6%
- 10%
- 13%

Personal computers per 1,000 people, 1996

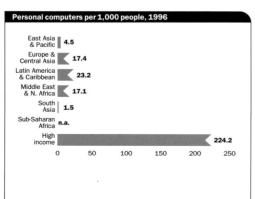

East Asia & Pacific	4.5
Europe & Central Asia	17.4
Latin America & Caribbean	23.2
Middle East & N. Africa	17.1
South Asia	1.5
Sub-Saharan Africa	n.a.
High income	224.2

0   50   100   150   200   250

Personal computers per 1,000 people, 1996

	Economies	GNP $ millions 1996	Population millions 1996	GNP per capita $ 1996
Less than 5.0	24	1,784,033	2,936	610
5.0–19.9	22	1,452,966	564	2,580
20.0–49.9	21	2,067,302	566	3,650
50.0 –149.9	19	8,252,732	334	24,740
150.0 or more	19	15,411,763	596	25,860
No data	105	540,819	758	710

Economy	Private investment % of GDFI[a] 1996	Stock market capitalization $ millions 1997	Central government overall deficit[b] % of GDP 1995	Military expenditures % of GNP 1995	Electricity consumption per capita kwh 1995	Telephone mainlines per 1,000 people 1996	Personal computers per 1,000 people 1996	Paved roads % of total 1996
Afghanistan	..	..	..	..	..	1	..	13.3
Albania	..	..	-9.0	1.1	623	19	..	30.0
Algeria	74.8	..	..	3.2	513	44	3.4	68.9
American Samoa	..	..	..	..	..	..	..	..
Andorra	..	..	..	..	..	423	..	..
Angola	68.9	..	..	3.0	60	5	..	25.0
Antigua and Barbuda	89.9	..	..	..	..	299	..	..
Argentina	85.8	59,252	-1.1	1.7	1,519	174	24.6	29.1
Armenia	33.6	7	..	0.9	811	154	..	100.0
Aruba	..	..	..	..	..	390	..	..
Australia	..	311,988	-2.5	2.5	8,033	519	311.3	38.7
Austria	..	33,953	-5.2	0.9	5,800	466	148.0	100.0
Azerbaijan	..	..	..	2.8	1,806	85	..	..
Bahamas, The	..	..	-2.6	..	..	278	..	57.4
Bahrain	..	..	-6.7	5.4	7,399	241	66.8	75.8
Bangladesh	62.5	4,551	..	1.7	57	3	..	7.2
Barbados	87.1	766	..	0.8	..	370	57.5	95.9
Belarus	..	..	..	0.8	2,451	208	..	70.1
Belgium	..	119,831	-3.9	1.7	6,752	465	167.3	..
Belize	66.6	..	-5.0	1.6	..	133	27.8	19.0
Benin	61.7	..	..	1.2	43	6	..	20.0
Bermuda	..	..	..	..	..	758	..	..
Bhutan	..	28	-3.2	..	..	3	..	60.7
Bolivia	41.9	114	-2.5	2.3	356	47	..	5.5
Bosnia and Herzegovina	..	..	..	..	397	90	..	52.3
Botswana	..	326	2.8	5.3	..	48	6.7	23.5
Brazil	86.2	255,478	-9.4	1.7	1,610	96	18.4	9.3
Brunei	..	..	..	6.0	5,270	263	28.7	34.7
Bulgaria	85.0	7	-5.3	2.8	3,415	313	295.2	91.9
Burkina Faso	57.9	..	..	2.9	..	3	..	16.0
Burundi	15.7	..	-3.7	4.4	..	2	..	7.1
Cambodia	68.6	..	..	3.1	..	1	..	7.5
Cameroon	95.5	..	0.2	1.9	196	5	..	12.5
Canada	..	486,268	-3.7	1.7	15,147	602	192.5	..
Cape Verde	11.9	..	..	1.0	..	64	..	78.0
Cayman Islands	..	..	..	..	..	..	..	..
Central African Republic	41.8	..	..	2.5	..	3	..	..
Chad	35.8	..	..	3.1	..	1	..	0.8
Channel Islands	..	..	..	..	..	..	..	..
Chile	80.0	72,046	2.5	3.8	1,698	156	45.1	13.8
China	47.0	206,366	-1.8	2.3	637	45	3.0	..
Hong Kong, China	86.8	449,381	..	..	4,850	547	150.5	100.0
Colombia	47.8	19,530	-0.5	2.6	948	118	23.3	11.9
Comoros	63.9	..	..	..	..	8	..	76.5
Congo, Dem. Rep.	..	..	0.0	0.3	132	1	..	..
Congo, Rep.	91.4	..	..	2.9	207	8	..	9.7
Costa Rica	75.1	782	-2.9	0.6	1,348	155	..	17.0
Côte d'Ivoire	69.1	914	..	..	159	9	1.4	9.7
Croatia	59.6	581	-0.9	10.5	2,074	309	20.9	81.5
Cuba	..	..	..	1.6	818	32	..	55.9
Cyprus	..	2,355	-1.5	5.8	3,033	485	40.9	57.1
Czech Republic	..	12,786	0.4	2.3	4,654	273	53.2	100.0
Denmark	..	71,688	-2.0	1.8	5,975	618	304.1	100.0
Djibouti	56.9	..	..	4.5	..	13	1.7	12.6
Dominica	61.0	..	..	..	..	264	..	50.4
Dominican Republic	66.5	..	0.8	1.4	588	83	..	49.4
Ecuador	78.3	1,946	0.0	3.7	600	73	3.9	13.3
Egypt, Arab Rep.	59.1	20,830	0.3	5.7	896	50	5.8	78.1
El Salvador	78.0	450	-0.1	1.1	507	56	..	19.9
Equatorial Guinea	99.5	..	..	1.6	..	9	..	21.8
Eritrea	52.7	..	..	..	..	5	..	21.8
Estonia	80.2	..	0.0	1.1	3,022	299	6.7	53.2
Ethiopia	63.9	..	-5.9	2.2	22	3	..	15.0
Faeroe Islands	..	..	..	..	..	473	63.8	..
Fiji	..	..	-3.4	1.7	..	88	..	49.2
Finland	..	63,078	-9.8	2.0	12,785	549	182.1	64.0
France	..	591,123	-6.5	3.1	5,892	564	150.7	100.0
French Guiana	..	..	..	..	..	289	..	..
French Polynesia	..	..	..	..	..	224	..	..
Gabon	72.0	..	..	2.6	737	32	6.3	8.2
Gambia, The	63.1	..	3.7	4.6	..	19	..	35.4
Georgia	73.7	..	..	2.4	1,057	105	..	93.5
Germany	..	670,997	-1.8	..	5,527	538	233.2	99.1
Ghana	26.3	1,492	-2.6	1.4	318	4	1.2	24.1
Greece	..	34,164	-9.6	5.5	3,259	509	33.4	91.8
Greenland	..	..	..	..	..	379	103.4	..
Grenada	78.5	..	..	2.3	..	248	..	61.3
Guadeloupe	..	..	..	..	..	396	..	..
Guam	..	..	..	..	..	457	..	..
Guatemala	81.3	168	-0.7	1.3	264	31	2.8	27.6
Guinea	57.7	..	..	1.5	..	2	0.3	16.5
Guinea-Bissau	32.5	..	..	2.8	..	7	..	10.3
Guyana	38.5	..	..	1.3	..	60	..	7.4
Haiti	27.6	..	..	2.9	32	8	..	24.3
Honduras	62.7	338	..	1.4	333	31	..	20.3
Hungary	..	14,975	..	1.5	2,682	261	44.1	43.1
Iceland	..	1,210	-4.5	..	16,011	573	205.2	25.9
India	66.1	128,466	-6.0	2.4	339	15	1.5	50.2
Indonesia	60.5	29,105	2.2	1.8	263	21	4.8	45.5
Iran, Islamic Rep.	..	17,008	1.4	2.6	1,059	95	32.7	50.0
Iraq	..	..	..	..	1,396	33	..	86.0
Ireland	..	12,243	-2.0	1.3	4,139	395	145.0	94.1
Isle of Man	..	..	..	..	..	..	..	..
Israel	..	45,268	-4.7	9.6	4,836	446	117.6	100.0
Italy	..	258,160	-7.6	1.8	4,163	440	92.3	100.0
Jamaica	..	1,887	..	0.8	2,049	142	4.6	70.7
Japan	..	3,088,850	-1.5	1.0	6,937	489	128.0	74.1
Jordan	77.1	5,446	1.1	7.7	1,139	60	7.2	100.0
Kazakhstan	98.8	..	..	0.9	3,106	118	..	80.5
Kenya	44.5	1,846	-3.4	2.3	123	8	1.6	13.9
Kiribati	..	..	..	..	..	26	..	..
Korea, Dem. Rep.	..	..	..	28.6	261	49	..	6.4
Korea, Rep.	76.0	41,881	0.3	3.4	3,606	430	131.7	76.1
Kuwait	..	18,817	..	11.6	13,185	232	74.1	80.6
Kyrgyz Republic	87.5	5	..	0.7	1,666	75	..	91.1
Lao PDR	..	..	..	4.2	..	6	1.1	13.8
Latvia	89.3	148	-4.2	0.9	1,789	298	7.9	38.3
Lebanon	71.8	..	-15.7	3.7	1,224	149	24.3	95.0
Lesotho	36.8	..	6.4	1.9	..	9	..	17.9
Liberia	..	..	..	..	..	2	..	6.2
Libya	..	..	..	6.0	3,569	59	..	57.2
Liechtenstein	..	..	..	..	..	..	..	..

Economy	Private investment % of GDFI[a] 1996	Stock market capitalization $ millions 1997	Central government overall deficit[b] % of GDP 1995	Military expenditures % of GNP 1995	Electricity consumption per capita kwh 1995	Telephone mainlines per 1,000 people 1996	Personal computers per 1,000 people 1996	Paved roads % of total 1996
Lithuania	86.3	900	-5.3	0.5	1,711	268	6.5	87.6
Luxembourg	..	32,692	4.1	0.7	12,198	593	..	100.0
Macao	93.8	..	..	..	..	367	94.2	100.0
Macedonia, FYR	..	..	..	3.3	2,443	170	..	63.8
Madagascar	42.5	..	-1.6	0.9	..	3	..	11.6
Malawi	84.3	..	..	1.6	..	4	..	18.5
Malaysia	69.8	93,608	2.3	3.0	1,953	183	42.8	75.1
Maldives	..	..	-9.4	..	..	63	12.3	..
Mali	54.4	..	..	1.8	..	2	..	12.1
Malta	..	472	-3.7	1.1	3,393	484	80.6	..
Marshall Islands	..	..	..	..	..	0	..	..
Martinique	..	..	..	..	..	425	..	..
Mauritania	68.3	..	..	3.2	..	4	5.3	11.3
Mauritius	64.8	1,676	-1.2	0.4	..	162	31.9	93.1
Mayotte	..	..	..	..	..	48	..	..
Mexico	79.1	156,595	-0.5	1.0	1,305	95	29.0	37.4
Micronesia, Fed. Sts.	..	..	..	..	..	65	..	17.7
Moldova	78.5	..	..	2.1	1,517	140	2.6	87.3
Monaco	..	..	..	..	..	..	..	100.0
Mongolia	..	..	-3.5	2.4	..	39	..	7.8
Morocco	57.8	12,177	..	4.3	407	45	1.7	50.4
Mozambique	65.3	..	..	5.4	67	3	0.8	18.7
Myanmar	60.6	..	-4.1	..	52	4	..	12.2
Namibia	62.2	473	-4.5	2.1	..	54	12.7	12.1
Nepal	67.8	208	-4.6	0.9	39	5	..	41.5
Netherlands	..	378,721	-4.9	2.1	5,374	543	232.0	90.1
Netherlands Antilles	..	..	..	..	3,950	374	..	..
New Caledonia	..	..	..	..	..	241	..	..
New Zealand	..	38,288	0.4	1.3	8,504	499	266.1	58.1
Nicaragua	38.6	..	-0.6	2.2	272	26	..	10.1
Niger	50.6	..	..	1.2	..	2	..	7.9
Nigeria	62.5	3,646	..	0.8	85	4	4.1	18.8
Northern Mariana Islands	..	..	..	..	..	329	..	..
Norway	..	57,423	1.6	2.7	23,892	555	273.0	72.0
Oman	..	2,673	-10.1	16.7	2,891	86	10.9	30.0
Pakistan	52.5	10,966	-4.8	6.1	304	18	1.2	57.0
Palau	..	..	..	..	..	..	..	..
Panama	83.8	831	2.9	1.4	1,089	122	..	33.6
Papua New Guinea	85.8	..	-4.1	1.4	..	11	..	3.5
Paraguay	83.4	383	1.2	1.4	683	36	..	9.5
Peru	82.9	17,586	-1.3	1.7	525	60	5.9	10.1
Philippines	81.1	31,361	0.6	1.5	337	25	9.3	..
Poland	81.9	12,135	-2.0	2.3	2,324	169	36.2	65.4
Portugal	..	38,954	-5.5	2.6	2,857	375	60.5	86.0
Puerto Rico	..	..	..	..	..	336	..	100.0
Qatar	..	..	..	4.4	8,734	239	62.7	90.0
Reunion	..	..	..	..	..	340	..	..
Romania	73.8	61	-2.5	2.5	1,603	140	5.3	51.0
Russian Federation	91.1	128,207	-4.4	11.4	4,172	175	23.7	78.8
Rwanda	70.0	..	-7.4	5.2	..	3	..	9.1
Samoa	..	..	..	..	..	55	..	42.0
São Tomé and Principe	35.8	..	..	..	..	20	..	68.1
Saudi Arabia	..	40,961	..	13.5	3,906	106	37.2	42.7
Senegal	70.3	..	..	1.6	91	11	7.2	29.3
Seychelles	67.9	..	-8.1	..	..	200	..	62.9
Sierra Leone	64.4	..	-6.1	6.1	..	4	..	11.0
Singapore	..	150,215	14.3	4.7	6,018	513	216.8	97.4
Slovak Republic	..	1,826	..	3.0	4,075	232	186.1	98.5
Slovenia	26.7	663	..	1.5	4,710	333	47.8	82.0
Solomon Islands	..	..	..	..	..	18	..	2.5
Somalia	..	..	..	..	..	2	..	11.8
South Africa	..	232,069	-5.9	2.2	3,874	100	37.7	41.5
Spain	..	242,779	-7.2	1.6	3,594	392	94.2	99.0
Sri Lanka	..	2,096	-8.3	4.6	208	14	3.3	40.0
St. Kitts and Nevis	84.9	..	1.1	..	..	382	..	42.5
St. Lucia	49.2	..	..	..	..	235	0.6	5.2
St. Vincent and the Grenadines	78.6	..	-0.3	..	..	171	..	30.7
Sudan	..	..	..	6.6	37	4	0.7	36.3
Suriname	..	..	..	3.0	..	132	..	26.0
Swaziland	63.4	1,642	..	2.6	..	22	..	28.2
Sweden	..	247,217	-11.1	2.8	14,096	682	214.9	76.1
Switzerland	..	402,104	-1.0	1.6	6,916	640	408.5	..
Syrian Arab Republic	..	..	-1.7	7.2	698	82	1.4	23.0
Tajikistan	..	..	..	3.7	2,367	42	..	82.7
Tanzania	..	..	..	1.8	52	3	..	4.2
Thailand	77.6	23,538	2.9	2.5	1,199	70	16.7	97.5
Togo	78.2	..	..	2.3	..	6	..	31.6
Tonga	..	..	..	..	..	67	..	27.0
Trinidad and Tobago	88.0	1,405	0.2	1.7	2,817	166	19.2	51.1
Tunisia	51.0	4,263	-3.2	2.0	661	64	6.7	78.9
Turkey	81.4	61,090	-4.1	4.0	1,057	224	13.8	25.0
Turkmenistan	..	..	..	1.7	1,109	74	..	81.2
Uganda	63.9	..	..	2.3	..	2	0.5	..
Ukraine	..	..	..	2.9	2,785	181	5.6	95.0
United Arab Emirates	..	..	0.2	4.8	7,752	302	65.5	100.0
United Kingdom	..	1,740,246	-5.3	3.0	5,081	528	192.6	100.0
United States	..	8,484,433	-2.2	3.8	11,571	640	362.4	60.8
Uruguay	71.1	266	-1.3	2.4	1,574	209	22.0	90.0
Uzbekistan	..	128	..	3.8	1,731	76	..	87.3
Vanuatu	..	..	..	..	..	26	..	23.9
Venezuela	31.5	14,581	-3.7	1.1	2,518	117	21.1	39.4
Vietnam	76.3	..	..	2.6	146	16	3.3	25.1
Virgin Islands (U.S.)	..	..	..	..	..	561	..	..
West Bank and Gaza	..	..	..	..	..	36	..	..
Yemen, Rep.	67.6	..	-5.5	15.7	99	13	..	8.1
Yugoslavia, FR (Serb./Mont.)	..	..	..	..	2,921	197	..	58.3
Zambia	48.7	229	-7.2	2.8	574	9	..	18.3
Zimbabwe	90.4	1,969	-10.7	4.0	738	15	6.7	47.4

.. Not available.

Note: Figures in italics are for years other than those specified; 0 or 0.0 means zero or less than half the unit shown and not known more precisely.

a. Gross domestic fixed investment. b. Includes grants.

Global Links

Global economic integration—a topic of much current debate—increases the ability of individuals and firms to undertake economic transactions with residents of other countries. Critics and proponents generally agree that the world is more integrated now than 50 years ago, but they disagree on whether integration is an opportunity or a danger and whether increasing integration is a strategic choice or an inevitable consequence—for better or worse—of economic and technical change. How much more integrated is the world? Which countries have been included and which have been left out? Have new, market-based links (investment) replaced old, official ones (aid)? The answers to these questions are important for shaping future development strategies, and the answers depend on how integration is measured.

In a fully integrated world, there would be no official barriers to negotiating and executing economic transactions—anywhere. And residents of one economy would face no higher transactions costs in a foreign market than in a domestic one. An integrated world is also better able to diversify risk and to provide insurance against disasters, both natural and humanmade.

Integration can be measured by the reduction of barriers to economic transactions—barriers that begin at borders with tariffs and nontariff barriers but that are buttressed by a wide range of domestic policies and practices. Integration can also be measured by evaluating economic outcomes—the volume of trade or capital flows, for example, or the pattern of product or asset prices across countries.

Ultimately, the value of integration must be assessed by its effects on people's lives. An integrated global economy may be more efficient, but it also may be less comfortable for many people. The continuing debate over tariff reductions reflects a deep suspicion that the benefits of globalization have been oversold. Concerns about environmental and social protection will also have to be resolved as globalization proceeds. Better measures of policies and their outcomes can help to inform this debate. The indicators shown in the *Atlas* focus on outcomes.

Interactions Économiques Mondiales

Objet de bien des débats à l'heure actuelle, l'intégration économique mondiale donne aux individus et aux entreprises la possibilité accrue de réaliser des transactions économiques avec les résidents d'autres pays. Critiques et partisans de cette évolution s'accordent généralement sur le fait que le monde d'aujourd'hui est plus intégré qu'il y a 50 ans, mais pas sur la question de savoir si cette intégration est une chance ou un risque, et si le renforcement de l'intégration est un choix stratégique ou une conséquence inéluctable — pour le meilleur ou pour le pire — de l'évolution économique et technique. Dans quelle mesure le monde est-il plus intégré ? Quels pays ce processus a-t-il inclus ou laissé de côté ? Les anciennes formes de relations officielles (l'aide) ont-elles fait place à de nouvelles formes, fondées sur le marché (l'investissement) ? Les réponses à ces questions sont importantes pour l'élaboration des stratégies de développement futures, mais elles dépendent de la manière dont l'intégration est mesurée.

Dans un monde totalement intégré, il n'y aurait pas de barrières officielles à la négociation et à la conclusion de transactions économiques, où que ce soit. Et les résidents d'un pays n'auraient pas à subir des coûts de transaction plus élevés sur un marché étranger que sur leur propre marché. Dans un monde intégré, l'investisseur est également mieux à même de répartir les risques et de se prémunir contre des catastrophes, d'origine naturelle ou humaine.

L'intégration peut se mesurer à la réduction des facteurs qui font obstacle aux transactions économiques ; commençant aux frontières, avec les barrières tarifaires et non tarifaires, ces obstacles sont encore renforcés par toute une série de politiques et pratiques en vigueur dans les pays. L'intégration peut également se mesurer au niveau des résultats économiques observés : par exemple, le volume des échanges commerciaux ou des flux de capitaux, ou la physionomie des prix des produits ou des actifs d'un pays à l'autre.

En dernière analyse, c'est aux effets qu'elle a sur la vie des individus qu'il convient de mesurer l'intérêt de l'intégration mondiale. Une économie mondiale intégrée est peut-être plus efficace, mais elle peut aussi rendre la vie plus difficile pour beaucoup de gens. Le débat dont continue de faire l'objet la question des réductions tarifaires témoigne du fait que beaucoup ont le net sentiment que les bienfaits de la mondialisation ont été surestimés. Un autre point à résoudre à mesure que celle-ci s'instaurera a trait aux préoccupations concernant la protection sociale et la sauvegarde de l'environnement. De meilleurs moyens d'évaluation des politiques et de leurs effets peuvent contribuer à éclairer le débat sur ces questions. Les indicateurs figurant dans l'*Atlas* se concentrent sur ces effets.

Integración Mundial

La integración económica mundial –un tema del que se habla mucho hoy día– aumenta la capacidad de los individuos y las empresas para realizar transacciones económicas con los residentes de otros países. Tanto los detractores como los defensores de este proceso coinciden en general en que el mundo está más integrado hoy día que hace 50 años, pero se muestran en desacuerdo cuando tratan de valorar si la integración representa una oportunidad o un peligro, y si la intensificación del proceso es una opción estratégica o una consecuencia inevitable –para bien o para mal– del cambio económico y tecnológico. ¿Hasta qué punto está integrado el mundo? ¿Qué países se han integrado y cuáles han quedado excluidos? ¿Han sustituido los nuevos vínculos basados en el mercado (inversión) a los antiguos vínculos oficiales (asistencia)? Las respuestas a estos interrogantes son importantes para conformar las futuras estrategias de desarrollo, y dependen de cómo se mida la integración.

En un mundo plenamente integrado no habría obstáculos oficiales para negociar y ejecutar transacciones económicas –en ningún lugar. Además, los residentes de un país no incurrirían en costos mucho mayores en una transacción exterior que en una nacional. Asimismo, un mundo integrado está en mejores condiciones de diversificar el riesgo y ofrecer seguridad frente a una catástrofe, ya sea natural o provocada por el hombre.

La integración puede medirse por la reducción de los obstáculos a las transacciones económicas, obstáculos que comienzan en las fronteras con las barreras arancelarias y no arancelarias, y que se refuerzan con una amplia gama de políticas y prácticas de carácter interno. También puede medirse evaluando los resultados económicos: el volumen de comercio o de flujos de capital, por ejemplo, o la estructura de precios de los productos o los activos en los distintos países.

En última instancia, el valor de la integración debe determinarse en función de sus efectos en la vida humana. Una economía mundial integrada puede ser más eficiente, pero también más incómoda para muchas personas. El debate permanente sobre la reducción de los aranceles refleja una profunda sospecha de que se han exagerado los beneficios de la globalización. A medida que avanza este proceso, habrá que resolver también algunas inquietudes en materia de protección ambiental y social. Una cuantificación más exacta de las políticas y sus resultados puede ayudar a arrojar luz sobre este debate. Los indicadores del *Atlas* se refieren sobre todo a los resultados.

Net private capital flows per capita, 1996

Net private debt and nondebt flows to developing economies, including commercial bank lending, bonds, other private credits, foreign direct investment, and portfolio equity investment, divided by population.

Flux nets de capitaux privés par habitant, 1996

Flux nets de capitaux privés générateurs et non générateurs de dette à destination des pays en développement, y compris les prêts des banques commerciales, les obligations, les autres crédits du secteur privé, les investissements étrangers directs et les investissements de portefeuille, divisés par la population.

Flujos netos de capital privado per cápita, 1996

Flujos privados de deuda y no relacionados con ésta a los países en desarrollo, incluidos los préstamos, bonos y otros créditos privados de bancos comerciales, la inversión extranjera directa y las inversiones de cartera en capital accionario, divididos por la población.

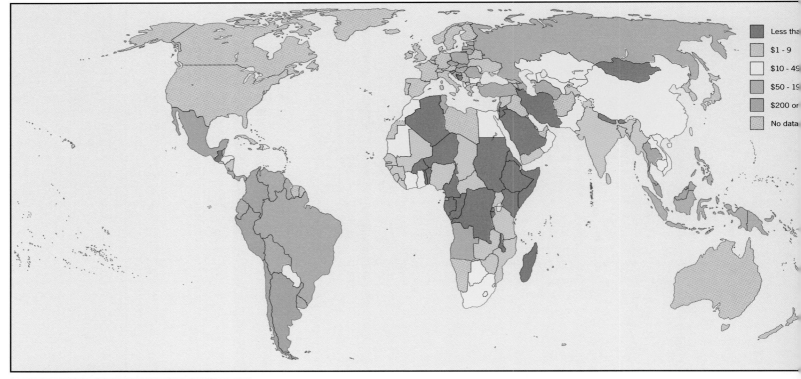

Legend:
- Less tha[n]
- $1 - 9
- $10 - 49
- $50 - 19[9]
- $200 or [more]
- No data

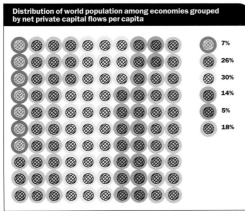

Distribution of world population among economies grouped by net private capital flows per capita

- 7%
- 26%
- 30%
- 14%
- 5%
- 18%

Net private capital flows, 1996 and 1997, $ billions

Region	1996	1997
East Asia & Pacific	101.3	89.1
Europe & Central Asia	35.0	41.2
Latin America & Caribbean	95.6	94.4
Middle East & N. Africa	2.0	14.0
South Asia	8.7	9.1
Sub-Saharan Africa	4.4	8.1

0   20   40   60   80   100   120

● 1996 ○ 1997

Net private capital flows per capita, 1996, $

	Economies	GNP $ millions 1996	Population millions 1996	GNP per capita $ 1996
Less than $1	27	258,744	393	660
$1–$9	32	614,205	1,506	410
$10–$49	29	1,353,718	1,685	800
$50–$199	31	1,964,671	822	2,390
$200 or more	18	1,210,500	305	3,960
No data	73	24,107,777	1,043	23,120

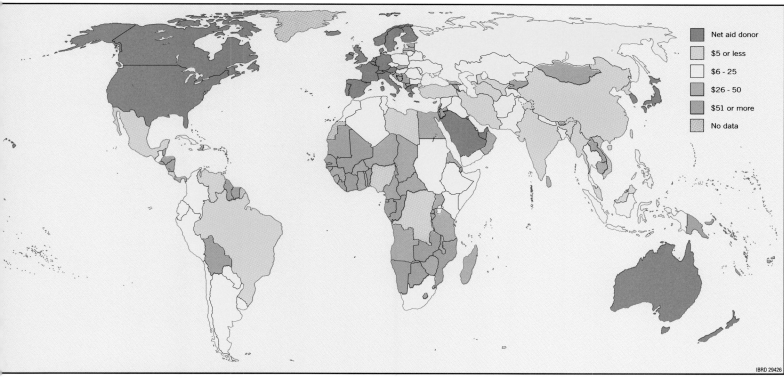

Net aid donor
$5 or less
$6 - 25
$26 - 50
$51 or more
No data

IBRD 29426

Net concessional loans and grants received by a country divided by its midyear population.

Flux nets d'aide par habitant, 1996

Total net des dons et prêts concessionnels officiels reçus par un pays, divisé par sa population en milieu d'année.

Flujos netos de asistencia per cápita, 1996

Donaciones y préstamos oficiales netos en condiciones concesionarias recibidos por un país, divididos por la población de mediados de año.

Distribution of world population among economies grouped by net aid flows per capita

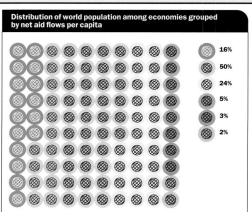

16%
50%
24%
5%
3%
2%

Net aid flows per capita, 1996, $

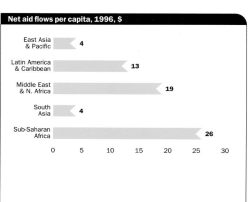

East Asia & Pacific — 4
Latin America & Caribbean — 13
Middle East & N. Africa — 19
South Asia — 4
Sub-Saharan Africa — 26

0   5   10   15   20   25   30

Net aid flows per capita, 1996, $

	Economies	GNP $ millions 1996	Population millions 1996	GNP per capita $ 1996
Net aid donor	27	23,215,476	897	25,880
$5 or less	23	3,465,585	2,880	1,200
$6–$25	47	2,266,361	1,411	1,610
$26–$50	30	230,186	295	780
$51 or more	63	241,973	187	1,300
No data	20	90,034	84	1,070

Economy	Trade in goods and services % of GDP PPP[a] 1996	Manufactured exports % of total merchandise exports 1996	Net private capital flows[b] $ millions 1996	Foreign direct investment % of GDP 1996	Net aid flows % of GNP 1996	Net aid flows per capita $ 1996	International tourism Receipts $ millions 1996	International tourism Arrivals thousands 1996
Afghanistan	..	..	..	..	..	9	1	4
Albania	..	..	92	3.4	8.1	68	11	56
Algeria	15.0	4	–72	0.0	0.7	11	16	605
American Samoa	..	..	..	..	..	..	9	19
Andorra	..	..	..	..	..	..	..	..
Angola	29.3	..	753	4.5	15.8	49	9	8
Antigua and Barbuda	54.4	..	..	5.0	2.5	182	..	..
Argentina	14.0	30	14,417	1.5	0.1	8	4,572	4,286
Armenia	14.0	..	18	1.0	18.2	78	1	..
Aruba	..	..	..	–5.9	1.5	258	553	641
Australia	34.0	30	..	1.6	‡	‡	8,703	4,165
Austria	71.6	88	..	1.7	‡	‡	14,004	17,090
Azerbaijan	16.3	..	601	16.5	3.0	14	158	145
Bahamas, The	96.2	..	..	3.1	..	1	1,378	1,669
Bahrain	182.5	16	..	–0.5	1.1	9	300	1,757
Bangladesh	8.3	..	92	0.0	3.9	10	32	166
Barbados	31.1	51	239	0.7	0.0	17	712	447
Belarus	26.3	..	7	0.1	0.4	7	48	234
Belgium	..	..	..	..	‡	‡	5,893	5,829
Belize	43.8	13	21	2.3	3.0	81	75	143
Benin	15.9	..	2	0.1	13.5	52	29	147
Bermuda	..	..	..	..	..	–66	505	390
Bhutan	..	40	–2	0.0	23.0	87	5	5
Bolivia	12.0	16	571	6.4	13.3	112	160	375
Bosnia and Herzegovina	..	..	0	..	..	184	..	..
Botswana	..	..	66	1.5	1.7	55	178	707
Brazil	10.2	54	28,384	1.3	0.1	3	2,469	2,140
Brunei	..	1	..	..	..	11	38	837
Bulgaria	23.8	..	300	1.2	1.9	20	450	2,795
Burkina Faso	9.8	..	0	0.0	16.5	39	23	136
Burundi	4.2	..	0	0.1	18.1	32	1	27
Cambodia	..	..	290	9.4	14.5	44	118	260
Cameroon	13.0	8	–28	0.4	4.9	30	52	101
Canada	58.5	63	..	1.1	‡	‡	8,868	17,286
Cape Verde	46.6	..	17	2.8	28.7	309	10	37
Cayman Islands	..	..	..	..	..	..	394	373
Central African Republic	8.6	43	5	0.5	16.1	50	5	29
Chad	5.7	..	18	1.5	26.9	46	10	8
Channel Islands	..	..	..	..	..	..	..	..
Chile	18.9	15	6,803	5.5	0.3	14	918	1,450
China	7.1	84	50,100	4.9	0.3	2	10,200	22,765
Hong Kong, China	247.6	92	..	..	0.0	2	10,836	11,703
Colombia	9.5	34	7,739	3.9	0.3	7	909	1,254
Comoros	20.2	..	2	0.9	17.4	79	9	25
Congo, Dem. Rep.	6.9	..	2	0.0	2.8	4	5	37
Congo, Rep.	70.6	2	–7	0.3	22.9	159	4	27
Costa Rica	34.4	24	387	4.5	–0.1	–2	689	781
Côte d'Ivoire	32.0	..	160	0.2	9.9	67	89	237
Croatia	59.9	72	915	1.8	0.7	28	2,100	2,649
Cuba	..	..	..	..	..	6	1,350	999
Cyprus	29.9	52	..	1.0	0.6	41	1,670	1,950
Czech Republic	46.3	84	4,894	2.6	0.2	12	4,075	17,000
Denmark	73.7	59	..	0.4	‡	‡	3,425	1,794
Djibouti	..	..	5	1.0	..	157	4	20
Dominica	99.5	49	19	8.3	19.4	582	30	62
Dominican Republic	28.3	77	366	3.0	0.8	13	1,755	1,926
Ecuador	16.3	9	816	2.3	1.5	22	281	500
Egypt, Arab Rep.	14.8	32	1,434	0.9	3.3	37	3,200	3,528
El Salvador	22.5	41	48	0.2	3.1	55	76	283
Equatorial Guinea	22.6	..	376	131.8	12.8	76	2	..
Eritrea	..	..	0	..	..	43	..	417
Estonia	77.4	68	191	3.5	1.4	42	470	600
Ethiopia	6.8	..	–205	0.1	14.3	15	46	107
Faeroe Islands	..	3	..	..	..	..	..	..
Fiji	46.8	36	–6	0.5	2.3	56	311	340
Finland	70.1	83	..	0.9	‡	‡	1,601	894
France	45.4	79	..	1.4	‡	‡	28,357	62,406
French Guiana	..	60	..	..	..	..	..	..
French Polynesia	..	..	..	..	..	1,833	280	164
Gabon	45.5	2	–114	–1.1	2.6	112	4	136
Gambia, The	11.9	..	11	2.2	13.4	34	22	77
Georgia	9.6	..	40	0.2	7.1	59	..	..
Germany	55.1	87	..	–0.1	‡	‡	16,496	15,205
Ghana	15.3	..	477	1.9	10.5	37	239	298
Greece	27.9	50	..	0.7	‡	‡	3,660	8,987
Greenland	..	4	..	..	..	..	..	..
Grenada	46.5	..	19	6.8	3.7	107	59	108
Guadeloupe	..	47	..	..	..	..	466	625
Guam	..	..	..	..	..	..	1,415	1,363
Guatemala	12.2	31	5	0.5	1.4	20	284	520
Guinea	13.1	..	41	0.6	7.8	44	1	94
Guinea-Bissau	14.2	..	1	0.4	67.5	164	..	..
Guyana	54.3	..	83	11.3	21.7	172	46	102
Haiti	12.6	..	4	0.2	14.4	51	81	150
Honduras	42.5	31	65	1.9	9.2	60	81	257
Hungary	41.4	68	1,618	4.4	0.4	18	2,246	20,674
Iceland	62.9	11	..	0.1	‡	‡	154	201
India	4.5	74	6,404	0.7	0.6	2	3,027	2,288
Indonesia	13.6	51	18,030	3.5	0.5	6	6,087	5,034
Iran, Islamic Rep.	9.6	..	–352	..	0.1	3	165	465
Iraq	..	..	..	..	..	18	13	345
Ireland	121.6	82	..	3.5	‡	‡	3,003	5,282
Isle of Man	..	..	..	..	..	..	..	..
Israel	47.5	91	..	1.7	0.4	389	2,800	2,097
Italy	39.6	89	..	0.3	‡	‡	28,673	32,853
Jamaica	53.7	69	191	4.0	1.4	24	1,092	1,162
Japan	26.1	95	..	0.0	‡	‡	4,078	2,114
Jordan	36.6	49	–119	0.2	7.2	119	744	1,103
Kazakhstan	19.6	..	615	1.5	0.6	8	..	..
Kenya	17.9	..	–104	0.1	6.8	22	474	717
Kiribati	..	..	..	1.8	17.1	161	1	3
Korea, Dem. Rep.	..	..	..	..	..	2	..	127
Korea, Rep.	46.7	92	..	0.5	‡	‡	5,430	3,684
Kuwait	45.8	5	..	..	..	..	109	33
Kyrgyz Republic	13.6	38	46	2.6	13.9	51	5	13
Lao PDR	16.5	..	104	5.6	18.2	72	50	93
Latvia	41.1	61	331	6.5	1.6	32	182	97
Lebanon	36.0	..	740	0.6	1.8	57	715	420
Lesotho	..	..	38	3.2	8.7	53	19	108
Liberia	..	..	17	..	..	74	..	..
Libya	..	..	..	..	..	2	6	88
Liechtenstein	..	..	..	..	..	..	..	56

Economy	Trade in goods and services % of GDP PPP[a] 1996	Manufactured exports % of total merchandise exports 1996	Net private capital flows[b] $ millions 1996	Foreign direct investment % of GDP 1996	Net aid flows % of GNP 1996	Net aid flows per capita $ 1996	International tourism Receipts $ millions 1996	International tourism Arrivals thousands 1996
Lithuania	46.6	60	469	2.0	1.2	24	345	832
Luxembourg	..	..	..	..	†	†	295	712
Macao	..	95	..	..	..	1	3,225	4,890
Macedonia, FYR	..	..	8	0.7	5.3	53	..	..
Madagascar	10.0	14	5	0.2	9.1	27	65	83
Malawi	16.8	7	-3	0.0	23.2	50	7	232
Malaysia	70.2	76	12,096	4.5	-0.5	-22	3,926	7,138
Maldives	63.1	..	10	2.6	11.5	128	265	339
Mali	19.9	..	23	0.9	19.4	51	20	50
Malta	95.1	..	397	5.8	0.3	193	618	1,054
Marshall Islands	..	..	..	..	64.1	1,279	2	6
Martinique	..	19	..	..	..	..	392	477
Mauritania	26.7	..	25	0.5	26.4	117	11	..
Mauritius	35.7	68	112	0.9	0.5	17	466	487
Mayotte	..	..	..	..	..	..	..	..
Mexico	26.1	78	23,647	2.3	0.1	3	6,934	21,405
Micronesia, Fed. Sts.	..	..	..	..	49.7	1,037	..	..
Moldova	41.4	23	115	2.2	2.1	9	59	33
Monaco	..	..	..	..	..	..	..	226
Mongolia	19.5	10	-15	0.5	21.3	81	21	153
Morocco	14.0	50	388	0.8	1.8	24	1,381	2,693
Mozambique	14.4	17	23	1.7	59.8	51	..	..
Myanmar	..	..	129	..	..	1	90	165
Namibia	..	..	..	4.2	5.7	119	265	405
Nepal	4.3	99	9	0.4	8.9	18	130	404
Netherlands	106.4	63	..	2.0	†	†	6,256	6,580
Netherlands Antilles	..	..	..	..	..	600	..	..
New Caledonia	..	..	..	..	..	2,011	109	91
New Zealand	45.0	29	..	0.4	†	†	2,444	1,529
Nicaragua	19.4	34	41	2.3	57.1	212	54	303
Niger	7.4	..	-24	0.0	13.2	28	17	17
Nigeria	21.5	..	706	4.3	0.6	2	85	822
Northern Mariana Islands	..	..	..	..	..	..	670	729
Norway	80.3	23	..	2.5	†	†	2,404	2,746
Oman	45.4	14	69	0.4	0.6	28	99	435
Pakistan	10.0	84	1,936	1.1	1.4	7	146	369
Palau	..	..	..	..	..	..	..	44
Panama	111.0	20	301	2.9	1.1	33	343	362
Papua New Guinea	33.0	..	414	4.4	8.0	87	68	56
Paraguay	29.3	17	202	2.3	1.0	20	236	425
Peru	13.0	16	5,854	5.9	0.7	17	535	515
Philippines	21.3	84	4,600	1.7	1.0	12	2,701	2,049
Poland	26.5	74	5,333	3.3	0.6	22	8,400	19,410
Portugal	43.1	86	..	0.6	†	†	4,265	9,730
Puerto Rico	..	..	..	..	..	..	1,898	3,065
Qatar	60.4	24	..	..	..	2	..	263
Reunion	..	21	..	..	..	..	258	346
Romania	16.8	77	1,814	0.7	0.6	10	20	136
Russian Federation	19.8	..	7,454	0.6	0.3	8	5,542	14,587
Rwanda	12.9	..	1	0.1	51.2	100	1	1
Samoa	..	..	4	2.3	18.4	189	39	73
São Tomé and Principe	..	..	0	0.0	114.7	347	2	2
Saudi Arabia	41.2	..	..	-1.5	..	†	1,308	3,458
Senegal	16.1	50	34	0.9	11.6	68	147	263
Seychelles	..	0	26	5.8	3.7	248	102	131
Sierra Leone	22.8	..	5	0.5	21.2	42	10	46
Singapore	316.0	84	..	10.0	0.0	0	7,916	6,608
Slovak Republic	52.2	68	1,265	1.5	0.7	26	673	951
Slovenia	74.0	90	1,219	1.0	0.4	41	1,210	832
Solomon Islands	41.2	..	17	5.7	11.9	110	13	11
Somalia	..	..	0	..	..	9	..	10
South Africa	20.7	49	1,417	0.1	0.3	10	1,995	4,944
Spain	36.8	78	..	1.1	†	†	27,414	41,295
Sri Lanka	21.5	73	123	0.9	3.6	27	168	302
St. Kitts and Nevis	54.4	..	16	6.9	3.0	171	297	238
St. Lucia	46.6	32	39	6.5	7.0	245	..	..
St. Vincent and the Grenadines	38.6	..	19	12.1	10.0	238	58	58
Sudan	..	..	0	..	..	8	7	65
Suriname	101.0	..	..	-6.4	17.9	257	14	21
Swaziland	..	..	13	1.2	2.9	33	38	305
Sweden	87.2	80	..	2.2	†	†	3,683	2,376
Switzerland	89.8	94	..	1.2	†	†	8,891	10,600
Syrian Arab Republic	19.6	..	77	0.6	1.4	16	1,478	888
Tajikistan	26.9	..	16	0.8	5.6	19	..	..
Tanzania	..	..	143	2.6	15.6	29	322	310
Thailand	31.3	73	13,517	1.3	0.5	14	8,664	7,192
Togo	19.5	..	0	0.0	12.0	39	8	58
Tonga	..	4	2	1.1	17.4	329	13	25
Trinidad and Tobago	53.7	39	343	5.9	0.3	13	74	282
Tunisia	30.2	80	697	1.6	0.7	14	1,436	3,885
Turkey	17.5	74	5,635	0.4	0.1	4	5,962	7,966
Turkmenistan	32.8	..	355	2.5	0.5	5	..	..
Uganda	6.3	..	114	2.0	11.3	35	100	205
Ukraine	35.0	..	395	0.8	0.9	7	202	814
United Arab Emirates	135.7	..	..	..	†	†	..	1,768
United Kingdom	46.3	82	..	2.8	†	†	19,296	25,293
United States	19.4	78	..	1.0	†	†	64,373	46,325
Uruguay	22.8	36	499	0.9	0.3	16	599	2,152
Uzbekistan	12.4	..	431	0.2	0.4	4	..	..
Vanuatu	38.6	..	28	13.1	13.8	181	50	46
Venezuela	19.0	12	4,244	2.7	0.1	2	846	759
Vietnam	17.7	..	2,061	6.4	4.0	..	87	1,607
Virgin Islands (U.S.)	..	..	..	..	..	..	811	375
West Bank and Gaza	..	..	..	..	..	..	..	..
Yemen, Rep.	56.3	1	100	1.7	4.9	17	42	74
Yugoslavia, FR (Serb./Mont.)	..	49	..	..	..	64	43	162
Zambia	26.1	..	33	1.7	18.6	67	60	264
Zimbabwe	19.8	30	42	0.8	5.2	33	219	1,743

.. Not available.

† Net aid donor.

Note: Figures in italics are for years other than those specified; 0 or 0.0 means zero or less than half the unit shown and not known more precisely.

a. Purchasing power parity; see the technical notes to the *Economy* section. b. Data are shown for low- and middle-income economies only.

People

Demographic data (population, life expectancy, and infant mortality) are World Bank estimates and are a combination of observed values and interpolated and projected estimates. The midyear population estimate includes all residents regardless of legal status or citizenship. Refugees not permanently settled in the country of asylum are considered to be part of the population of their country of origin. The average annual population growth rate is calculated as the exponential change for the period indicated.

Consumption per capita is private consumption expenditure divided by the midyear population. Growth in private consumption per capita is calculated using the least-squares method. Private consumption includes the consumption expenditures of individuals, households, and nonprofit, nongovernmental organizations. It includes expenditures on food, clothing, rent, health care, education, transportation, and consumer durables.

Malnutrition refers to the percentage of children under five whose weight for age is more than two standard deviations below the average for the reference population. The data are from the United Nations Children's Fund and the Subcommittee on Nutrition of the United Nations Administrative Committee on Co-ordination. Net female primary enrollment ratio compares the number of girls of official school age enrolled in primary school to the number of official school-age girls in the population. Enrollment data are from the United Nations Educational, Scientific, and Cultural Organization. Female labor force estimates are from the International Labour Organization.

Environment

Land area is the country's total area, excluding the area under inland bodies of water. Data on land area and forests are from the Food and Agriculture Organization. Definitions of forest area vary among countries.

Energy data are from the International Energy Agency and refer to commercial forms of energy. Traditional fuels, although important in some developing economies, are not included in these estimates. Gross domestic product (GDP, in 1987 U.S. dollars) per kilogram of oil equivalent is an indicator of energy efficiency.

Data on water are based on estimates from the World Resources Institute and cover domestic, industrial, and agricultural use. Available freshwater resources refer to internal renewable resources. Water use includes nonrenewable water from aquifers and desalination plants and therefore can exceed total internal renewable resources.

Carbon dioxide emissions are those stemming from the burning of fossil fuels and the manufacture of cement. Data on emissions are based on several sources, as reported by the World Resources Institute.

Economy

Gross national product (GNP) is a broad measure of an economy's performance; it is the value of the final output of goods and services produced by the residents of an economy plus net primary income from nonresident sources. U.S. dollar values are obtained from domestic currencies using a three-year weighted average of the official exchange rate (the Atlas method). For the few countries where the official exchange rate does not reflect the effective rate applied to foreign transactions, an alternative conversion factor is applied. The GNP per capita growth rate is calculated from constant price data in the local currency, using the least-squares method. Data on national accounts and inflation are from World Bank and OECD data files.

GNP per capita in international dollars is converted at purchasing power parity (PPP) rates. PPP is defined as the number of units of a country's currency required to buy the same amounts of goods and services in the domestic market as $1 would buy in the United States. The 1996 data are based on surveys carried out since 1993 or on regression estimates. PPP data are from the International Comparison Programme.

The share of agriculture in GDP is calculated from value added estimates of agriculture. The share of investment in GDP is based on gross domestic investment (including changes in inventories). Inflation is measured by the overall price change for all goods and services included in GDP. Inflation rates are calculated using the least-squares method. The current account balance is the sum of net exports of goods, services, income, and current transfers; these data are from World Bank and International Monetary Fund (IMF) data files. External debt data is from the World Bank's Debtor Reporting System, and is debt owed to nonresidents repayable in foreign currency, goods, or services. Total external debt is the sum of public, publicly guaranteed, and private nonguaranteed long-term debt, use of IMF credit, and short-term debt.

States and Markets

Private investment—that is, outlays by the private sector on additions to fixed assets—is often estimated as a residual of gross domestic investment less consolidated public investment. These data are from World Bank data files. Stock market capitalization is the end-year share price times the number of shares outstanding in each country's stock market. These data are from the International Finance Corporation's Emerging Markets Database.

The overall budget deficit is current and capital revenue and official grants received less total expenditures and lending minus repayments. These data are from World Bank and IMF data files.

Military expenditures for NATO countries are based on the NATO definition, which covers military-related expenditures of the defense ministry (including recruiting, training, construction, and the purchase of military supplies and equipment) and other ministries. Civilian-related expenditures of the defense ministry are excluded. Military assistance is included in the expenditures of the donor country, and purchases of military equipment on credit are included at the time the debt is incurred, not at the time of payment. Data for other countries generally cover expenditures of the ministry of defense (excluding expenditures on public order and safety, which are classified separately). Data on military expenditures are from the U.S. Arms Control and Disarmament Agency.

Electricity consumption measures the production of power plants and combined heat and power plants less distribution losses and own use by heat and power plants. Paved roads are roads that have been sealed with asphalt or similar road-building materials. Data on electricity consumption are from the International Energy Agency; data on paved roads are from the International Road Federation. Telephone mainlines per 1,000 people provide a measure of telephone density. Telephone mainlines refer to the telephone lines connecting a customer's equipment to the public switched telephone network. Estimates of the number of personal computers (PCs) are derived from an annual questionnaire by the International Telecommunication Union (ITU), supplemented by other sources. Data on telephone mainlines and PCs are from the ITU.

Global Links

Trade of goods and services as a share of GDP is the sum of exports and imports of goods and services divided by GDP. Manufactured exports include chemicals, basic manufactured goods, and machinery and transport equipment but exclude nonferrous metals. Trade data are from the IMF and the United Nations Conference on Trade and Development. Net private capital flows consist of private debt and nondebt flows. Private debt flows include commercial bank lending, bonds, and other private credits. Private nondebt flows are foreign direct investment and portfolio equity investment. Foreign direct investment is net inflows of investment to acquire a lasting management interest (10 percent or more of voting stock) in an enterprise operating in an economy other than that of the investor. It is the sum of equity capital, reinvestment of earnings, other long-term capital, and short-term capital as shown in the balance of payments. Data on net private capital flows are drawn from World Bank and IMF data files.

Aid data cover net concessional flows to developing countries from members of the Development Assistance Committee of the OECD and from multilateral development agencies. These data are from the OECD. International tourism receipts are expenditures by international inbound visitors, including payments to national carriers for international transport. International tourist arrivals is the number of visitors who travel to another country for less than one year. These data are from the IMF and the World Tourism Organization.

For a fuller discussion of issues of data quality and measurement problems for the above indicators, see *About the data* sections in the relevant tables in *World Development Indicators 1998* or in the *World Development Indicators* CD-ROM.

Note

Data are shown for economies as they were constituted in 1996, and historical data are revised to reflect current political arrangements. Exceptions are noted throughout the tables.

On July 1, 1997, China resumed its exercise of sovereignty over Hong Kong. Data for China do not include Hong Kong, China, or Taiwan, China, unless otherwise noted.

Data for the Democratic Republic of Congo (Congo, Dem. Rep. in the table listings) refer to the former Zaire. For clarity, this edition also uses the formal name of the Republic of Congo (Congo, Rep. in the table listings).

Data are shown whenever possible for the individual countries formed from the former Czechoslovakia—the Czech Republic and the Slovak Republic.

Data are shown for Eritrea whenever possible, but in most cases before 1992 Eritrea is included in the data for Ethiopia.

Data for Germany refer to the unified Germany unless otherwise noted.

Data for Jordan refer to the East Bank only unless otherwise noted.

In 1991 the Union of Soviet Socialist Republics (U.S.S.R) was dissolved into 15 countries (Armenia, Azerbaijan, Belarus, Estonia, Georgia, Kazakhstan, Kyrgyz Republic, Latvia, Lithuania, Moldova, Russian Federation, Tajikistan, Turkmenistan, Ukraine, and Uzbekistan). Whenever possible, data are shown for the individual countries.

Data for the Republic of Yemen refer to that country from 1990 onward; data for previous years refer to the former People's Democratic Republic of Yemen and the former Yemen Arab Republic unless otherwise noted.

Whenever possible, data are shown for the individual countries formed from the former Yugoslavia—Bosnia and Herzegovina, Croatia, the former Yugoslav Republic of Macedonia, Slovenia, and the Federal Republic of Yugoslavia (Serbia and Montenegro).

Population

Les données démographiques (population, espérance de vie et mortalité infantile), fruit d'estimations de la Banque mondiale, sont une combinaison de valeurs observées et d'estimations obtenues par interpolation et projection. L'estimation de la population en milieu d'année inclut tous les résidents du pays, indépendamment du statut juridique et de la citoyenneté. Les réfugiés qui ne sont pas établis à titre permanent dans le pays où ils ont trouvé asile sont comptés dans la population de leur pays d'origine. Le taux annuel moyen d'accroissement de la population est calculé comme l'évolution exponentielle pendant la période considérée.

La consommation par habitant est mesurée en termes de dépenses de consommation privée, divisée par la population en milieu d'année. Le taux de croissance de la consommation privée par habitant est calculé par la méthode des moindres carrés. La consommation privée recouvre les dépenses de consommation des individus, des ménages et des organismes non gouvernementaux à but non lucratif, en matière d'alimentation, d'habillement, de loyer, de soins de santé, d'éducation, de transport et de biens de consommation durables.

La malnutrition renvoie au pourcentage d'enfants âgés de moins de cinq ans dont le poids pour leur âge est inférieur de plus de deux écarts types à celui de la moyenne de la population de référence. Les données utilisées sont celles du Fonds des Nations Unies pour l'enfance et du Sous-Comité de la nutrition du Comité administratif de coordination des Nations Unies. Le taux net de scolarisation primaire féminine met en rapport le nombre des filles d'âge scolaire qui sont inscrites à l'école primaire et le nombre total des filles d'âge scolaire au sein de la population. Les données sur les effectifs scolarisés proviennent de l'Organisation des Nations Unies pour l'éducation, la science et la culture. Les estimations de la part des femmes dans la population active émanent du Bureau international du travail.

Environnement

La superficie des terres correspond à la superficie totale d'un pays moins la superficie des eaux intérieures. Les données sur la superficie des terres et les forêts proviennent de l'Organisation des Nations Unies pour l'alimentation et l'agriculture. La définition des zones boisées varie selon les pays.

Les données sur l'énergie proviennent de l'Agence internationale de l'énergie et concernent les formes commerciales d'énergie. Malgré le rôle considérable qu'ils jouent dans l'économie de certains pays en développement, les combustibles traditionnels ne sont pas pris en compte dans ces estimations. Le produit intérieur brut (PIB, en dollars des États-Unis de 1987) par kilogramme équivalent pétrole fournit un indicateur du rendement énergétique.

Les données relatives à l'eau reposent sur des estimations de l'Institut des ressources mondiales et couvrent les usages domestiques, industriels et agricoles. Les données sur les ressources en eau douce incluent les ressources intérieures renouvelables. Le volume total d'eau consommée comprend les ressources non renouvelables provenant des nappes aquifères et des usines de dessalement et peut donc dépasser le total des ressources intérieures renouvelables.

Les émissions de dioxyde de carbone prises en compte sont celles produites par les combustibles fossiles et la fabrication de ciment. Les données sur ces émissions font appel à plusieurs sources, recensées par l'Institut des ressources mondiales.

Économie

Le produit national brut (PNB) est une mesure d'ensemble de la performance économique d'un pays ; il représente la valeur de la production finale de biens et services assurée par les résidents du pays, plus les montants nets de revenu primaire versés par des non-résidents. Les valeurs en dollars des États-Unis sont obtenues par conversion de la valeur en monnaie nationale sur la base d'un taux de change officiel moyen pondéré sur trois ans (méthode de l'Atlas). Pour les quelques pays où le taux de change officiel ne correspond pas au taux de change effectif appliqué aux transactions avec l'étranger, on utilise un autre facteur de conversion. Le taux de croissance du PNB par habitant est calculé à partir de données exprimées en prix constants dans la monnaie nationale, par la méthode des moindres carrés. Les données sur les comptes nationaux et l'inflation proviennent des fichiers de données de la Banque mondiale et de l'OCDE.

Le PNB par habitant en dollars internationaux est obtenu par conversion sur la base de la parité des pouvoirs d'achat (PPA). La PPA est définie comme le nombre d'unités de la monnaie d'un pays nécessaire pour acheter sur le marché intérieur la même quantité de biens et services qu'un dollar permettrait d'acheter aux États-Unis. Les chiffres de 1996 ont été calculés à partir d'enquêtes réalisées depuis 1993 ou par analyse de régression. Les données établies sur la base des PPA proviennent du Projet de comparaison internationale des Nations Unies.

La part de l'agriculture dans le PIB est calculée à partir des estimations de la valeur ajoutée de l'agriculture. La part de l'investissement dans le PIB repose sur l'investissement intérieur brut (y compris les variations du niveau des stocks). L'inflation est mesurée en termes de variation de l'ensemble des prix de tous les biens et services pris en compte dans le PIB. Le taux d'inflation est calculé par la méthode des moindres carrés. Le solde des transactions courantes est la somme des exportations nettes de biens et de services, des revenus et des transferts courants ; ces données proviennent des fichiers de données de la

Banque mondiale et du Fonds monétaire international (FMI). Les données relatives à la dette extérieure proviennent du Système de notification de la dette extérieure à la Banque mondiale et correspondent aux créances sur des non-résidents remboursables en devises, en biens ou en services. La dette extérieure totale est la somme de la dette publique, de la dette à garantie publique, de la dette privée non garantie à long terme, du recours au crédit du FMI et de la dette à court terme.

État et Marché

L'investissement privé, c'est-à-dire les dépenses du secteur privé pour la formation de capital fixe, est souvent estimé par différence entre l'investissement intérieur brut et l'investissement du secteur public consolidé. Ces données proviennent des fichiers de données de la Banque mondiale. La capitalisation boursière est établie à partir du cours des actions en fin d'année, multiplié par le nombre d'actions en circulation sur le marché boursier du pays considéré. Ces données proviennent de la Base de données sur les marchés émergents de la Société financière internationale.

Le déficit budgétaire global est la différence entre, d'une part, les recettes courantes, les recettes en capital et les dons publics reçus et, d'autre part, les dépenses totales et les prêts moins les remboursements. Ces données proviennent des fichiers de données de la Banque mondiale et du FMI.

Les données sur les dépenses militaires, dans le cas des pays de l'OTAN, reposent sur la définition établie par cette organisation, qui englobe les dépenses à caractère militaire effectuées par le ministère de la défense (y compris les opérations de recrutement, les activités de formation, les travaux de construction et l'achat de matériel et de fournitures militaires) et les autres ministères. Les dépenses à caractère civil du ministère de la défense en sont exclues. L'aide militaire est incluse dans les dépenses du pays donateur, et les achats de matériel militaire effectués à crédit sont répertoriés à la date à laquelle la créance est contractée, et non pas à la date de remboursement. Dans le cas des autres pays, les données englobent généralement les dépenses du ministère de la défense (à l'exclusion de celles destinées à la sécurité et à l'ordre publics, qui sont classées séparément). Les données sur les dépenses militaires proviennent de la U.S. Arms Control and Disarmament Agency.

La consommation d'électricité correspond à la production des centrales électriques et des centrales électrocalogènes, déduction faite des pertes de distribution et de l'autoconsommation des centrales électrocalogènes. Les routes revêtues sont les routes recouvertes d'asphalte ou de matériaux analogues. Les données sur la consommation d'électricité proviennent de l'Agence internationale de l'énergie et celles relatives aux routes revêtues, de la Fédération routière internationale. Le nombre de lignes téléphoniques principales pour mille habitants mesure la densité de l'équipement téléphonique. Par lignes téléphoniques principales, on entend les lignes téléphoniques raccordant le matériel d'un abonné au réseau téléphonique public commuté. Les estimations du nombre d'ordinateurs individuels sont tirées d'un questionnaire annuel administré par l'Union internationale des télécommunications (UIT), complété par d'autres sources. Les données relatives aux lignes téléphoniques principales et aux ordinateurs individuels proviennent de l'UIT.

Interactions Économiques Mondiales

Les échanges de biens et services en pourcentage du PIB correspondent à la somme des exportations et des importations de biens et services, divisée par le PIB. Les exportations de biens manufacturés englobent les produits chimiques, les articles manufacturés de base, les machines et le matériel de transport, mais excluent les métaux non ferreux. Les données sur les échanges proviennent du FMI et de la Conférence des Nations Unies sur le commerce et le développement. Les flux nets de capitaux privés recouvrent les flux au titre de la dette privée et les flux de capitaux privés non associés à la dette. Les flux au titre de la dette privée recouvrent les prêts des banques commerciales, les obligations et autres crédits du secteur privé. Les flux privés non associés à la dette sont les investissements étrangers directs nets et les investissements de portefeuille. Les investissements étrangers directs sont des investissements effectués pour acquérir des droits durables (représentant au moins 10 % des actions donnant droit de vote) sur une entreprise fonctionnant dans un pays autre que celui de l'investisseur. Ils représentent la somme des capitaux propres, des bénéfices réinvestis, des autres capitaux à long terme et des capitaux à court terme, comme indiqué dans la balance des paiements. Les données sur les flux nets de capitaux privés proviennent des fichiers de données de la Banque mondiale et du FMI.

Les données sur l'aide prennent en compte les apports concessionnels nets aux pays en développement émanant des pays membres du Comité d'aide au développement de l'OCDE et des organismes d'aide multilatérale au développement. Elles proviennent de l'OCDE. Les recettes du tourisme international sont les dépenses effectuées dans le pays d'accueil par les visiteurs internationaux, y compris le paiement de leurs transports internationaux aux compagnies nationales de transport. Les arrivées de touristes internationaux représentent le nombre de visiteurs qui se rendent dans un autre pays pour une période de moins d'un an. Ces données proviennent du FMI et de l'Organisation mondiale du tourisme.

Pour un examen plus approfondi des questions de qualité des données et des problèmes de mesure des indicateurs, voir les sections relatives aux données des tableaux correspondants figurant dans *World Development Indicators 1998* ou sur le *World Development Indicators* CD-ROM.

Note

Les données sont présentées pour les pays tels qu'ils étaient constitués en 1996, et les chiffres se rapportant aux périodes antérieures ont été modifiés sur la base des situations politiques actuelles. Les exceptions sont signalées en note aux divers tableaux.

Le 1er juillet 1997, la Chine a recouvré l'exercice de sa souveraineté sur Hong Kong. Sauf indication contraire, les données pour la Chine ne comprennent pas Hong Kong (Chine) ou Taïwan (Chine).

Les données sur la République démocratique du Congo (dans les tableaux, « Congo, Dem. Rep. ») se rapportent à l'ex-Zaïre. Pour plus de clarté, le nom officiel de la République du Congo est également utilisé dans la présente édition (dans les tableaux, « Congo, Rep. »).

Dans la mesure du possible, on a présenté des données distinctes pour la République tchèque et pour la République slovaque, que couvrait antérieurement la Tchécoslovaquie.

Dans la mesure du possible, des données sont présentées séparément pour l'Érythrée, mais les données antérieures à 1992 présentées pour l'Éthiopie incluent, dans la plupart des cas, l'Érythrée.

Sauf indication contraire, les données sur l'Allemagne portent sur l'Allemagne unifiée.

Sauf indication contraire, les données sur la Jordanie se rapportent uniquement à la Rive orientale du Jourdain.

En 1991, l'Union des républiques socialistes soviétiques (URSS) a été scindée en 15 pays (Arménie, Azerbaïdjan, Bélarus, Estonie, Fédération de Russie, Géorgie, Kazakhstan, Lettonie, Lituanie, Moldova, Ouzbékistan, République kirghize, Tadjikistan, Turkménistan et Ukraine). Les données relatives à chaque pays ont été présentées dans la mesure du possible.

Les données présentées pour la République du Yémen ne couvrent pas les années antérieures à 1990 ; sauf indication contraire, les données indiquées pour ces années se rapportent à l'ex-République démocratique populaire du Yémen et à l'ex-République arabe du Yémen.

Dans la mesure du possible, on a présenté des données distinctes pour les pays que couvrait l'ex-Yougoslavie – Bosnie-Herzégovine, Croatie, ex-République yougoslave de Macédoine, Slovénie et République fédérative de Yougoslavie (Serbie et Monténégro).

Población

Los datos demográficos (población, esperanza de vida y mortalidad infantil) son estimaciones del Banco Mundial y consisten en una combinación de valores observados y estimaciones interpoladas y proyectadas. La estimación de la población a mediados del año comprende a todos los residentes, independientemente de su situación jurídica o su ciudadanía. Los refugiados que no se han establecido definitivamente en el país de asilo se consideran parte de la población de su país de origen. La tasa media de crecimiento anual de la población se calcula como la variación exponencial correspondiente al período indicado.

El consumo per cápita es el gasto en concepto de consumo privado dividido por la población a mediados del año. El aumento del consumo privado per cápita se calcula utilizando el método de mínimos cuadrados. En el consumo privado se incluyen los gastos de consumo de los individuos, los hogares y las organizaciones no gubernamentales sin fines de lucro. Se incluyen los gastos en alimentos, vestido, alquiler, atención de salud, educación, transporte, y artículos de consumo duraderos.

La malnutrición se refiere al porcentaje de niños menores de cinco años cuyo peso para la edad se encuentra más de dos desviaciones estándar por debajo del promedio para la población de referencia. Los datos provienen del Fondo de las Naciones Unidas para la Infancia y del Subcomité de Nutrición del Comité Administrativo de Coordinación de las Naciones Unidas. La tasa neta de matrícula de mujeres en la escuela primaria es una comparación entre el número de niñas en edad escolar oficial matriculadas en la escuela primaria y el número total de niñas en edad escolar oficial. Los datos sobre la matrícula provienen de la Organización de las Naciones Unidas para la Educación, la Ciencia y la Cultura. Las estimaciones sobre las mujeres en la población activa provienen de la Organización Internacional del Trabajo.

Medio Ambiente

La superficie terrestre es la superficie total de un país, excluida la parte del mismo cubierta por masas de agua continentales. Los datos sobre la superficie terrestre y los bosques provienen de la Organización de las Naciones Unidas para la Agricultura y la Alimentación. Las definiciones de lo que constituye una zona forestal varían de un país a otro.

Los datos sobre la energía provienen del Organismo Internacional de Energía y se refieren a las formas de ésta que están disponibles en el mercado. En las estimaciones no se toman en cuenta los combustibles tradicionales, aunque revisten importancia en algunos países en desarrollo. El PIB (en dólares de EE.UU. de 1987) por kilogramo de equivalente en petróleo es un indicador de la eficiencia del uso de la energía.

Los datos sobre el agua se basan en estimaciones del Instituto de Recursos Mundiales y se refieren al uso residencial, industrial y agrícola de este elemento. Los recursos disponibles de agua dulce se refieren a los recursos internos renovables. El uso del agua incluye el agua no renovable de los acuíferos y la proveniente de las plantas de desalinización del agua de mar y, por lo tanto, las cifras pueden ser mayores que las del total de recursos renovables internos.

Las emisiones de dióxido de carbono comprenden las procedentes de la quema de combustibles fósiles y la fabricación de cemento. Los datos sobre las emisiones se basan en varias fuentes señaladas por el Instituto de Recursos Mundiales.

Economía

El producto nacional bruto (PNB) es una medida amplia del desempeño de la economía de un país; representa el valor total de los bienes y servicios producidos por los residentes de un país más las entradas netas de ingreso primario provenientes de no residentes. Los valores en dólares de EE.UU. se obtienen a partir de las monedas nacionales aplicando un tipo de cambio oficial medio ponderado correspondiente a tres años (el método del Atlas). En el caso de los pocos países en que el tipo de cambio oficial no refleja el tipo real aplicado a las transacciones externas, se aplica otro factor de conversión. La tasa de crecimiento del PNB per cápita se calcula a partir de datos en precios constantes en la moneda nacional utilizando el método de mínimos cuadrados. Los datos sobre las cuentas nacionales y la inflación provienen de los archivos de datos del Banco Mundial y de la OCDE.

El PNB per cápita en dólares internacionales se convierte en función de la paridad de poder adquisitivo (PPA). La PPA se define como el número de unidades de la moneda de un país que se necesita para comprar en el mercado nacional la misma cantidad de bienes y servicios que se podría comprar con un dólar en Estados Unidos. Los datos correspondientes a 1996 se basan en estudios realizados a partir de 1993 o en estimaciones de regresión. Los datos relativos a la PPA provienen del Programa de Comparación Internacional.

La proporción de la agricultura en el PIB se calcula en base a estimaciones del valor agregado de la agricultura. La proporción de la inversión en el PIB se basa en la inversión interna bruta (incluidos los cambios en las existencias). La inflación corresponde a las variaciones globales de los precios de todos los bienes y servicios incluidos en el PIB. Las tasas de crecimiento de la inflación se han calculado utilizando el método de los mínimos cuadrados. La balanza de cuenta corriente es la suma de las exportaciones netas de bienes, servicios, ingreso y transferencias corrientes; estos datos provienen de los archivos de datos del Banco Mundial y el Fondo Monetario Internacional (FMI). Los datos sobre

la deuda externa provienen del Sistema de notificación de la deuda al Banco Mundial; dicha deuda es la contraída frente a entidades no residentes y es reembolsable en moneda extranjera, bienes o servicios. La deuda externa total es la suma de la deuda pública y con garantía pública a largo plazo, la deuda privada a largo plazo sin garantía, la utilización del crédito del FMI y la deuda a corto plazo.

Estados y Mercados

La inversión privada, es decir, los gastos del sector privado en concepto de adiciones a los activos fijos, a menudo se calcula como el residuo de la inversión interna bruta menos la inversión pública consolidada. Estos datos provienen de los archivos de datos del Banco Mundial. La capitalización del mercado de valores corresponde al precio de las acciones al final del período multiplicado por el número de valores en circulación en la bolsa de valores de cada país. Estos datos provienen de la Base de Datos sobre Mercados Emergentes de la Corporación Financiera Internacional.

El déficit fiscal global es el ingreso corriente y el ingreso de capital más las donaciones oficiales menos los gastos y préstamos totales menos los reembolsos. Estos datos provienen de los archivos de datos del Banco Mundial y el FMI.

Los gastos militares en los países miembros de la OTAN se basan en la definición de la OTAN, que cubre los gastos militares del ministerio de defensa (incluidos el reclutamiento, el entrenamiento, la construcción, y la adquisición de equipo y suministros militares) y otros ministerios. Se excluyen los gastos del ministerio de defensa relativos al sector civil. La asistencia militar se incluye en los gastos del país donante y las compras de equipo militar a crédito se incluyen en el momento en que la deuda es contraída, no al momento del pago. Los datos sobre otros países generalmente incluyen los gastos del ministerio de defensa (excluidos los gastos en seguridad y orden públicos, que se clasifican por separado). Los datos sobre gasto militar provienen del organismo de control de armamentos y de desarme de los Estados Unidos (U.S. Arms Control and Disarmament Agency).

El consumo de electricidad es una medida de la producción de las centrales de energía eléctrica y la producción combinada de las centrales térmicas y las centrales de energía eléctrica menos las pérdidas de transmisión y el propio uso de las centrales térmicas y las centrales de energía eléctrica. Carreteras pavimentadas son aquellas que han sido cubiertas con asfalto u otros materiales similares para la construcción de caminos. Los datos sobre el consumo de electricidad provienen del Organismo Internacional de Energía; los relativos a las carreteras pavimentadas se han tomado de la Federación Internacional de Carreteras. El número de líneas telefónicas principales por cada 1.000

personas indica la densidad de teléfonos. Líneas telefónicas principales son las que conectan el equipo del cliente a la red telefónica pública conmutada. Las estimaciones del número de computadoras personales provienen de un cuestionario anual preparado por la Unión Internacional de Telecomunicaciones (UIT) y son complementadas con datos de otras fuentes. Los datos sobre las líneas telefónicas principales y las computadoras personales provienen de la UIT.

Integración Mundial

El intercambio de bienes y servicios en proporción del PIB es la suma de las exportaciones e importaciones de bienes y servicios dividida por el PIB. En las exportaciones manufacturadas se incluyen los productos químicos, bienes manufacturados básicos, y maquinaria y equipo de transporte, pero se excluyen los metales no ferrosos. Los datos sobre comercio internacional provienen del FMI y la Conferencia de las Naciones Unidas sobre Comercio y Desarrollo. Los flujos netos de capital privado comprenden los flujos privados de deuda y los no relacionados con ésta. Los flujos privados de deuda incluyen los préstamos, bonos y otros créditos privados de bancos comerciales. Los flujos privados no relacionados con la deuda corresponden a la inversión extranjera directa y a las inversiones de cartera en capital accionario. La inversión extranjera directa corresponde a las afluencias netas de inversión destinadas a adquirir un control duradero de la gestión (10% o más de las acciones con derecho a voto) en una empresa que lleva a cabo sus operaciones en un país que no es el país del inversionista. Es la suma del capital social, la reinversión de las utilidades, otros tipos de capital a largo plazo y capital a corto plazo tal como aparece en la balanza de pagos. Los datos sobre flujos netos de capital privado provienen de los archivos de datos del Banco Mundial y el FMI.

Los datos sobre la asistencia comprenden los flujos netos de recursos en condiciones concesionarias de los países miembros del Comité de Asistencia para el Desarrollo de la OCDE y de organismos multilaterales de desarrollo con destino a los países en desarrollo. Estos datos provienen de la OCDE. Los ingresos provenientes del turismo internacional corresponden a los gastos incurridos por los visitantes extranjeros que entran a un país, incluidos los pagos a empresas nacionales de transporte internacional. La llegada de turistas extranjeros es el número de visitantes que viajan a otro país por un período inferior a un año. Estos datos provienen del FMI y la Organización Mundial de Turismo.

Para un examen más detenido de los problemas relacionados con la calidad de los datos y los problemas de cuantificación, véanse las explicaciones sobre los datos contenidas en los correspondientes cuadros de *World Development Indicators 1998* o en el *World Development Indicators* CD-ROM.

Nota

Los datos presentados corresponden a los países según éstos estaban constituidos en 1996, y los datos históricos han sido corregidos para indicar los sistemas políticos vigentes. Las excepciones se indican en los cuadros, según corresponda.

El 1 de julio de 1997 China recuperó el ejercicio de su soberanía sobre Hong Kong. En los datos sobre China no se incluyen Hong Kong, China, ni Taiwán, China, a menos que se indique lo contrario.

Los datos correspondientes a la República Democrática del Congo (Congo, Dem. Rep. en las listas de los cuadros) se refieren al ex Zaire. Para mayor claridad, en esta edición se utiliza también el nombre oficial de la República del Congo (Congo, Rep. en las listas de los cuadros).

En la medida de lo posible, se presentan datos por separado de los países que surgieron de la ex Checoslovaquia, a saber, la República Checa y la República Eslovaca.

Cuando ha sido posible, se han presentado datos relativos a Eritrea, pero, hasta 1992, la información sobre ésta se incluye en la de Etiopía.

Salvo indicación en contrario, los datos correspondientes a Alemania se refieren a la Alemania unificada.

Salvo indicación en contrario, los datos relativos a Jordania se refieren a la Ribera Oriental solamente.

En 1991, la Unión de Repúblicas Socialistas Soviéticas (URSS) se dividió oficialmente en 15 países (Armenia, Azerbaiyán, Belarús, Estonia, Federación de Rusia, Georgia, Kazajstán, Letonia, Lituania, Moldova, República Kirguisa, Tayikistán, Turkmenistán, Ucrania y Uzbekistán). En la medida de lo posible, se presentan datos por separado para cada país.

Los datos relativos a la República del Yemen se refieren a ese país a partir de 1990; los datos sobre años anteriores corresponden a la ex República Democrática Popular del Yemen y a la ex República Árabe del Yemen, a menos que se indique otra cosa.

En la medida de lo posible, se presentan datos por separado de los países surgidos de la antigua Yugoslavia: Bosnia y Herzegovina, Croacia, la ex República Yugoslava de Macedonia, Eslovenia, y la República Federativa de Yugoslavia (Serbia y Montenegro).

World Development Indicators 1998

The second annual edition of the World Bank's flagship statistical reference—*World Development Indicators 1998*. This award-winning publication provides an expanded view of the world economy for 148 countries—with chapters focusing on people, economy, environment, states and markets, world view, and global links as well as introductions highlighting recent research on major development issues. The 1998 edition includes some **key indicators for 1997**.

**April 1998 370 pages Stock no.
14124 (ISBN 0-8213-4124-3) $60.00**

**An award-winning series! Included in Choice Magazine's
34th annual Outstanding Academic Book list!**

Also Available on CD-ROM

This comprehensive database contains underlying time-series data for the *World Development Indicators* and *World Bank Atlas,* **now covering 1965-1996 for most indicators with some extending to 1997.** Powerful features allow you to generate maps and charts and download your results to other software programs.
Requires Windows 3.1.™

**April 1998 Individual Version: Stock no. 14125 (ISBN 0-8213-4125-1) $275.00
Network Version: Stock no. 14126 (ISBN 0-8213-4126-X) $550.00**

World Bank Atlas 1998

One of the Bank's most popular offerings, the *Atlas* is designed as a companion to the *World Development Indicators*. Tables, charts, and colorful maps address the development themes of people, economy, environment, states and markets, world view, and global links. This easy-to-use, book is an international standard in statistical compilations and an ideal reference for office or classroom. Text, maps, and references appear in English, French, and Spanish.

April 1998 64 pages Stock no. 14127 (ISBN 0-8213-4127-8) $20.00

World Bank Publications

For US customers, contact The World Bank, P.O. Box 960, Herdon, VA 20172-0960. Phone: (703) 661-1580, Fax: (703) 661-1501. Shipping and handling: US$5.00. For airmail delivery outside the US, charges are US$13.00 for one item plus US$6.00 for each additional item. Payment by US$ check drawn on a US bank payable to the World Bank or by VISA, MasterCard, or American Express. Customers outside the US may also contact their local World Bank distributor. To find the distributor in your country, consult the list on the last page. If no distributor is listed for your country, contact the World Bank directly.

Quantity	Title	Stock #	Price	Total Pri

Subtotal cost US$ _____

Shipping and handling US$ _____

Total US$ _____

❑ Bank check   ❑ VISA   ❑ MasterCard   ❑ American Express

_____
credit card account number

Expiration Date   Signature (required to validate all orders)

PLEASE PRINT CLEARLY

Name _____

Address _____

City _____

State _____   Postal Code _____

Country _____

Telephone _____